A WOMAN CALLED MOSES

A WOMAN CALLED MOSES

A Prophet for Our Times

Jean-Christophe Attias

Translated by Gregory Elliott

VERSO

London • New York

This work has been published with the help of the French
Ministry of Culture – Centre national du livre
Ouvrage publié avec le concours du Ministère français
chargé de la culture – Centre national du livre

This English-language edition published by Verso 2020
Originally published in French as *Moïse fragile*
© Alma Editeur 2015
Translation © Gregory Elliott 2020

1 3 5 7 9 10 8 6 4 2

Verso
UK: 6 Meard Street, London W1F 0EG
US: 20 Jay Street, Suite 1010, Brooklyn, NY 11201
versobooks.com

Verso is the imprint of New Left Books

ISBN-13: 978-1-78873-639-8
ISBN-13: 978-1-78873-641-1 (UK EBK)
ISBN-13: 978-1-78873-642-8 (US EBK)

British Library Cataloguing in Publication Data
A catalogue record for this book is available from the British Library

Library of Congress Cataloging-in-Publication Data
A catalog record for this book is available from the Library of Congress

Typeset in Garamond by Biblichor Ltd, Edinburgh
Printed and bound by CPI Group (UK) Ltd, Croydon, CR0 4YY

Contents

Preface

Behold, I will stand before thee upon the rock in Horeb; and thou shalt smite the rock, and there shall come water out of it, that the people may drink (Exod 17:6).

A book on Moses. The idea wasn't mine. It was suggested to me. It would never have occurred to me spontaneously. And, even when it came up, I wasn't easily persuaded. That said, I couldn't get it out of my mind, couldn't get free of it. Someone said 'Moses' to me and, curiously enough, Moses it was.

They could have said 'Abraham'; they could have said 'a book on Abraham'. Things would have been simpler then. It would have been out of the question. Exit Abraham – and by the back door. Abraham is the first of a line: a father. But he is also the most terrifying of fathers. When God asks him to sacrifice his son Isaac, he doesn't hesitate for a second over brandishing the sacrificial knife. And God respects him for it. The last straw. Abraham: unworthy father.

In any event, I'm not so fond of these stories of lineages and genealogies. We naively believe they can resolve all the issues of identity, major and minor, that trouble us. But the opposite is true. Father of all humanity, Adam was the father of Cain and Abel in the first instance. We know how that family turned out. Abraham was the father of Isaac, putative ancestor of Hebrews and Jews, but also of Ishmael, putative ancestor of Arabs and Muslims. Here again, two *frères ennemis*. That's not the end of it. Isaac would have two sons: Jacob, who continued the 'legitimate' line, and Esau, supposed forebear of Rome and Christianity.[1] Two more *frères ennemis*. Jacob himself begat a set of brothers who so hated one of their number – Joseph – that they planned to kill him at one stage, but finally sold him to merchants on their way to Egypt. It would seem that this is pretty much all our fathers are capable of engendering: *frères ennemis*.

Because your head is full of images of him, you might say to me: 'But Moses is at any rate a paternal figure!' Yes, precisely, a paternal figure – not a father. Moses had two sons. We know their names – Gershom and Eliezer – and that's about all. They did not have glorious careers and can boast no prestigious descendants. In this respect, Aaron – Moses's brother – was much more of a success: he founded an illustrious line of priests. And a little later, David – King David – didn't do badly: he was the first link in a glorious dynasty from which the Messiah would hail. Nothing of the sort in Moses's case.

Even as a 'paternal figure', and more so if by that we mean a 'bogeyman figure', Moses is not really up to it. Worse – or better, if you like – he was also (as we shall see) a 'maternal' figure. In Moses, there is as much of the soft touch as the firm hand. Don't be taken in by his fits of anger, his violence, the cruel punishments he is capable of inflicting on sinners. His great strength often consists in being able to reject force: the power of renunciation and abdication.

No, Moses was not a father, but a teacher. And that is not the same thing. He demands nothing of us by virtue of our blood. He speaks to our minds. He wants us to be his free pupils. Moses teaches us. He expects our adherence to what he teaches, but we remain free to refuse it. We never cease to be the sons of our fathers. But we can always reject the lessons of our teachers. By casting himself as a master and setting us up as his pupils, Moses makes us in turn masters of what he teaches us. And because he is no longer here to clarify 'what he meant by that', he leaves us free to interpret his oeuvre.

We shall always have the advantage over him that the commentary possesses over the source – especially (if some are to be believed) because Moses himself is not the true author of the works whose paternity is commonly attributed to him. He was at most the receiver and faithful transmitter of the word of Another. A Word that was transcribed, set down in writing: the Pentateuch* (the first five books of the Bible). And then another Word, one more fluid, more open, more alive, and always amenable to enrichment – the Word heard by the ear and transmitted exclusively via the mouth: the oral Tradition.

What's more, Moses, or his divine Inspirer, was not always crystal-clear. Their messages are sometimes ambiguous, contradictory, replete with omissions and things left unsaid. In them, light borders on darkness, is mysteriously combined with it. This disquieting zone of uncertainty is the hallowed ground of our freedom, as exegetes old or new.

So, 'a book on Moses'. Yes, ultimately, why not? But what kind of book? The book of a historian of Judaism? Rather, the book of a Jewish historian, which is quite different. The book of a historian who, because he is Jewish, is suddenly liberated from the constrictions, constraints and petty pedantries of his main discipline. And the book of a Jew who, because he is a historian, and though he is the inheritor of a centuries-old tradition, is not its slave or hidebound guardian.

Nor is this a study of the 'historical Moses', assuming he ever existed: I happily consign that solemn, pointless inquiry to those more austere and patient than I. Nor is it a cultural study of representations of Moses: the size of the task is off-putting and the fruits of such a labour might prove equally so. Nor, as readers can well imagine, is it a sacred history: no 'authorized' portrait, no pious image, is to be found here. I've never gone in for ingratiating deference, and I don't intend to start now.

So what, then? What book? What kind of book? To know, or decide, I had only to repeat the original question: why, once floated, did the idea of a book on Moses, which had never hitherto crossed my mind, refuse to leave me? Why, once someone had pronounced the name 'Moses', was Moses suddenly there? And why did I find myself incapable of escaping that presence? And, first up, where in fact was Moses – *my* Moses, since such, ultimately, is the subject of this book?

My own Moses was precisely where Moses wasn't. He was not to be found in the fire of miracles, the thunder of revelations, or the consecration of the Law. He was elsewhere, in gaps in the text, in the silence of words; in various mysterious, obscure moments of his implausible life story. He was where he stumbled, hesitated, gave up. He was where death stalked him, before finally striking. A man the contours of whose fate is unpredictable, always on the point of breaking apart, and ultimately doing so.

This Moses, who is more disturbing than reassuring, is not always easy to discern. He reveals himself by hiding; often we only see him from behind. Like God himself. We need to catch him in the shadows, at a distance, in the fold of words, in the hidden crevices of the text. We must go and seek him out, even if to do so is to invent him, and even if what we find has, in essence, been created by us.

This book is the record of an exegesis – parlous, groping, dogged – and the exegesis of a record – parlous, groping, dogged. I have utilized the rabbinical tradition as a staff, striking the rock of the biblical text to make the water of meaning spring from it. In so doing, I have shattered the rock, ruined the staff, and the water I have brought forth is not always of the purest.

In the process, I have taken the risk of falling out with everyone: with my historian colleagues, for having betrayed their method and ignored their lessons; with believers, for not having been able wholly to renounce irony. As to God, who does not exist, I remain sufficiently unreasonable to hope for his mercy.

Ault – Paris, December 2014

Note on the Translation

For the English edition of *Moïse fragile*, the Old and New Testaments are cited, with occasional modifications, in the Authorized Version (the King James Bible) and the Qur'an is cited in M. A. S. Abdel Haleem's translation (Oxford and New York: Oxford University Press, 2016). Rabbinical texts have been translated from the author's (re)translation into French of the Hebrew or Aramaic, except for the Palestinian recensions of the *Targum du Pentateuque*, translated by Roger Le Déaut (5 vols, Paris: Cerf, 1980–2008).

I have deliberately limited the number of notes. Endnotes either provide clarification or useful supplementary information, or they give short references to works other than the Bible and Qur'an cited in the text. Words and the names of persons followed by a superscript asterisk are the subject of a note in the glossary (pp. 159–70). Readers will find an indicative bibliography with full details at the end of the book. My system of transcription from the Hebrew does not aim to be scientific, but simply to facilitate reading by non-specialists.

Abbreviations Used for Books of the Bible

Old Testament
Genesis – Gen
Exodus – Exod
Numbers – Num
Leviticus – Lev
Deuteronomy – Deut
Joshua – Josh
I-II Samuel – I-II Sam
I-II Kings – I-II Kgs
I-II Chronicles – I-II Chr
Isaiah – Isa
Jonah – Jon
Malachi – Mal

New Testament
Matthew – Matt
I-II Corinthians – I-II Cor

The Life of Moses
according to the Pentateuch

Before setting out in Moses's footsteps, it might be useful to refresh our memories a bit. This summary is intended as a guide for readers unfamiliar with the biblical story or who have perhaps forgotten it. Obviously, it possesses no 'historical' value and does not adopt any of the various datings proposed – and contested – for the episodes it refers to. It simply records, in the occasionally erratic order in which they appear, most of the events recounted by the four relevant books of the Pentateuch: Exodus, Leviticus, Numbers and Deuteronomy. (The first – Genesis – is a history of the origins of the world and humanity and then, more specifically, of Abraham's posterity down to its settlement in Egypt. Accordingly, Moses does not feature in it.) When an episode is treated in detail in this book, reference is made to the relevant pages in parentheses.

[Exodus] *Early Years.* Amid mounting persecution of the children of Israel, enslaved in Egypt, Moses is born into a family of the tribe of Levi. Pharaoh commands that all newborn

Hebrew males should henceforth be cast into the Nile. Moses's mother (Jochebed) hides her son for three months and then abandons him to the river in a wicker basket. Moses is saved by Pharaoh's daughter, who entrusts him to a Hebrew wet nurse. This is none other than his biological mother, recommended to Pharaoh's daughter by Moses's sister, Miriam (pp. 25–37).

Having grown up at Pharaoh's court, Moses returns to his Hebrew brethren and discovers their woes. He kills an Egyptian who is beating a Hebrew and hides the body in the sand. He then tries to intervene in a dispute between two Hebrews. Rumours of his crime, and the threat of death looming over him, compel him to flee Egypt. He reaches Midian. At a well, he saves the daughters of a local priest (Jethro) from an attack by violent shepherds. He marries one of them (Zipporah) and has two sons with her (Gershom and Eliezer) (pp. 37–41).

While living a simple shepherd's life, Moses witnesses a strange phenomenon: he sees a burning bush that is not consumed by the flames. A divine voice addresses him from the bush, instructing him to assume leadership of Israel and free it from slavery. Moses tries to duck the mission, claiming not to be equal to the task and not to be a 'man of words' (pp. 16–20). God favours him with three miracles: he changes his staff into a snake and vice versa; he infects his hand (with leprosy?) and cures it; and he empowers him to change the water of the Nile into blood. Armed with these thaumaturgical faculties, and after God has given him an assistant and spokesman – his brother Aaron – Moses accepts the mission. He returns to Egypt, accompanied by his wife and children. On the way, in the night, God (or his messenger) threatens to kill Moses, whom Zipporah saves from certain death by proceeding to circumcise their (last?) son as a matter of urgency (pp. 51–76).

The Great Exodus. Moses and his brother Aaron endeavour to get Pharaoh to yield. They ask him to let the Hebrews depart on a three-day trek through the desert to sacrifice to their God. The initial effect of this request is a deterioration in the Hebrews' living and working conditions. God reveals himself once again to Moses, under the name of Yahweh – a name by which he had not previously made himself known to the Patriarchs.

Pharaoh does not give way, even though Moses and Aaron have vanquished the court magicians with a miracle: their staff turned into a big serpent. The magicians did the same with their staffs, but Aaron's snake swallowed the magicians'. Pharaoh's heart only grows harder. Nine successive plagues strike Egypt (sparing Israel): the waters of the Nile transformed into blood; frogs; lice; wild beasts; death of livestock; ulcers; hail; locusts; and darkness. Only after the tenth – the death of all Egypt's first-born – will the Hebrews be allowed to leave. They have celebrated the first Passover, each family having sacrificed a lamb with whose blood they daubed the uprights and lintels of their doors. The Exterminating Angel 'passed over' the houses thus marked out and the Hebrew first-born were spared (pp. 67–68).

The Hebrews leave Egypt, guided by a column of cloud and fire, enter the desert, and soon find themselves trapped between the Red Sea, whose shore they have just reached, and the Egyptian armies which Pharaoh, regretting his decision, has sent in pursuit of them. Moses raises his staff, the sea parts, and the Hebrews cross it without wetting their feet. Then the sea closes over the Egyptian troops, who are all drowned. Moses and the sons of Israel sing a hymn to the glory of the God of Israel, which is taken up by his sister Miriam and all the women.

In Sinai. The early stages of the Hebrews' trek to the Promised Land are peppered with incident. Thirsty, the people find water after three days, but the spring is bitter. It becomes sweet when Moses throws into it a piece of wood indicated to him by God. A little later, hunger torments the Hebrews, who are suddenly nostalgic for the fine dishes of Egypt. God causes a miraculous food – manna – to rain from the sky every morning, with a double ration on Friday (to keep the Shabbat*). They feed on it for forty years, until their arrival at the borders of Canaan. Then they are once again tormented by thirst. At God's command, Moses strikes a rock with his staff and water gushes out, which the people drink (p. 118).

Shortly afterwards, the Amalekites attack Israel. Stationed on a hill, Moses lifts his arms to heaven, with Aaron and Hur supporting him when he grows weary, and thus ensures victory for the Hebrews, fighting under the command of Joshua below. Jethro, having heard of the miracles performed on Israel's behalf, comes to join his son-in-law, accompanied by Zipporah and her two sons (pp. 39–40, 49 and 61–62). It is he who suggests to Moses an administrative and judicial arrangement that will release the prophet from the excessive duties weighing him down.

Having arrived in Sinai, the people prepare for the theophany – the manifestation of the divine presence – which is going to seal the Covenant*. On the third day, Moses summons the people to meet God. The people remain at the foot of the mountain. God then reveals the Decalogue* (or Ten Commandments).

Alarmed by the thunder, the flames, the sound of the trumpet and the smoking mountain, the people ask Moses to be the sole direct recipient of the Revelation. Thus, it is Moses who, in a private encounter, receives the remainder of the Law from God and then communicates it to the Hebrews. The Covenant is solemnly concluded by sacrifices, a reading of the Book of the Covenant, and a sprinkling of the people with sacrificial blood (pp. 68–69). Moses re-ascends the mountain. God imparts instructions for building a portable sanctuary that can be dismantled, which is to accompany the Hebrews in their wanderings; for making the clothes of Aaron and the priests; and for ordaining the latter. God gives Moses the two Tables* of the Law, the tablets of stone 'written by the finger of God'.

As Moses is slow in coming down the mountain, the people grow impatient and ask Aaron to make a replacement chief and god for them: the Golden Calf. Moses intercedes to appease God's anger and spare Israel from extermination. Finally descending, Moses breaks the Tables and punishes the people himself. He asks God's forgiveness (atonement) for the sin committed and suggests to him that, in the event of forgiveness being refused, he should erase him, Moses, from the 'book' of the Lord (pp. 77–92). The people resume their trek and it is no longer God who walks before them, but an angel. Moses asks God to see his Glory, but God only exhibits himself from behind. Moses carves two new Tables, re-ascends Sinai, and again speaks directly with God. When he returns, he is unaware that the skin on his face is shining. He will henceforth conceal his face behind a veil – except when talking with God or communicating God's teaching to the people (pp. 138–146).

The portable sanctuary is constructed, God takes possession of it, and his Glory fills it.

[Leviticus] God reveals to Moses the ordinances regarding sacrificial offerings. The priests assume office. But the sons of Aaron – Nadab and Abihu – offer God profane fire he had not commanded from them. Another fire immediately issues from God, which engulfs and kills them.

God reveals to Moses the laws of cleanliness: the clean and unclean animals, the purification of women who have just given birth, the treatment for human leprosy and leprosy in a house, cases of sexual impurity. God lays down ordinances for observing the Day of Atonement. He reveals the stipulations of the so-called law of holiness: proscription of the profane slaughter of animals, correct uses of blood, matrimonial and sexual prohibitions, various religious, moral and worship prescriptions, the principal cycles of the year and its solemn occasions, the sabbatical year, Jubilee.

Moses is led to condemn a blasphemer, the son of an Israelite woman and an Egyptian man, to be stoned to death (pp. 41–48).

[Numbers] Moses proceeds to an inventory of the twelve tribes, stipulates the order in which each must pitch camp as well as walk, and reveals various laws concerning life in the camp (exclusion of the unclean, the trial by ordeal of women suspected of adultery, Nazirites, etc.). After final instructions, the Hebrews resume their trek.

From Sinai to the Borders of the Land of Canaan. At Taberah they first give vent to their complaints. God grows angry and a fire begins to devour them, which Moses's intercession succeeds in extinguishing.

Soon, tired of eating manna and nostalgic once more for the dishes of Egypt, the Hebrews complain again. God becomes exceedingly irate and Moses is pained. He wonders how he will find meat for them, and tells God that he would rather die than continue to bear the heavy burden of this people. God appoints seventy elders, whom he graces with the gift of prophecy, to assist Moses. And the Hebrews will have meat: a flock of quails. However, they will be visited by death, in a place henceforth called Kivrot Ha-Ta'avah, 'the graves of greed' (pp. 94–99). Miriam and Aaron malign Moses, but he is confirmed by God as a prophet without peer. By way of punishment, Miriam is struck by leprosy (she is cured after seven days).

Moses sends twelve explorers into the land of Canaan. On their return, they describe it as an extraordinarily fertile country, but occupied by invincible peoples. Only two of the spies – Joshua and Caleb – seek to persuade Israel to undertake its conquest. The Hebrews lament and give up. Without Moses's intervention, they would be wiped out by God. Finally, the desert generation – the one born in Egypt, more than twenty years ago – is condemned to wander in the desert for forty years and to die there. Only their descendants will be able to enter Canaan. Israel rallies, launches an attack on Canaan against Moses's advice, and suffers a heavy defeat at Horma (pp. 110–116).

A man caught gathering wood on the Shabbat is brought before Moses, to whom God indicates the penalty to be imposed: he is stoned outside the camp by the whole community. Soon Korah, Dathan and Abiram are challenging the authority of Moses and Aaron and the latter's sacerdotal privileges. The rebels are consumed by fire. And only Aaron's intercession saves the community from the divine scourge that is beginning to kill them. God thus confirms Aaron's pre-eminence: the twelve princes of the tribes come to deposit their staffs in the tabernacle, and Aaron's alone miraculously produces blooms and fruit in one night.

At Kadesh Miriam dies, and the people are again without water. Moses strikes a rock twice with his staff (instead of speaking to it, as God had requested), and water gushes from it which the people drink. Because they did not trust in God, Moses and Aaron are condemned not to enter Canaan (pp. 116–120).

The King of Edom having refused Israel passage, it heads for the south of Canaan. Aaron dies on Mount Hor and his son Eliezer succeeds him as high priest. The Hebrews win a victory over the King of Arad. Continuing on their way, they once more grow impatient and rebel; God sends 'fiery serpents' from which they are saved by Moses's intercession. Near Nebo they join battle with two Amorite kings, Sihon and Og, whom they crush. The Hebrews are now encamped in the plains of Moab.

Balak, king of Moab, takes fright and asks the seer Balaam to curse Israel. Balaam drags his feet before finally setting out, although this journey does not seem to please God. A divine messenger lays an ambush, from which he is saved only by the wisdom of his she-donkey.

Rather than cursing Israel, Balaam ends up blessing it, compelled so to do by God. Balak and Balaam return to their respective homes (pp. 70–74). This is when Moab's daughters lead the Hebrews into debauchery and idolatry. Only the reaction of Aaron's grandson Phinehas, who spears a couple formed of a Hebrew man and a Midianite woman, arrests the divine scourge that has descended on Israel.

Various ordinances of the Law are spelt out as regards sacrifices, war, and the rules for settling the people of Israel in lands already conquered (in Transjordan, east of the Jordan River) or still to be conquered. The daughters of Zelophehad, having come to claim their father's share of the territory of Canaan (he died without male heirs), obtain satisfaction: consulted by Moses, God grants their request. Four decades of wandering in the desert are about to end. The desert generation has perished. God invites Moses, before he dies, to see the land given to Israel, which he will not enter. Joshua is named as his successor. He will lead the conquest.

[Deuteronomy] *Moses's Final Moments.* Addressing his people, Moses recaps the history of the past forty years: the departure from Sinai, the episode of the explorers, the long treks through the desert, the victories over Sihon and Og, the conquest and distribution of Transjordan, and God's refusal to allow him to cross the Jordan, obliging him to hand over to Joshua (pp. 111–114).

Moses urges his people to obey the laws of Sinai, not to succumb to the enticements of idolatry, and to acknowledge the greatness of their God. In a second speech, he recalls the promulgation of the Ten Commandments and Israel's defeatist attitude (pp. 99–101). He enjoins Israel to love God and obey his commandments; to have no pity for the idolatrous peoples it is going to dispossess; and to place itself exclusively under the protection of the Everlasting God. He recalls the episode of the Golden Calf and other insurgencies. He reveals various prescriptions regarding the future Sanctuary and worship; the punishment to be meted out to idolaters; prohibited funeral rites; clean and unclean foods; tithes; the sabbatical year; the three pilgrimage festivals; various ordinances on kings, Levites, cities of refuge, the conduct of war, marriage, divorce, the levirate, the duty to erase the memory of Amalek, and so on.

It only remains for Israel to choose between life and death, between the blessings that will reward observance of the commandments and the scourges that will punish their transgression. Moses hands over to his successor Joshua, sings a hymn and blesses the tribes. He ascends to the summit of Mount Pisgah, gazes from afar at the land he will not enter, and dies aged 120. His burial site is unknown (pp. 14–16, 103–110).

I

The Prophet's Wounded Body

I have little time for heroes. My personal pantheon is sometimes empty, sometimes overpopulated, and my enthusiasms ephemeral or changing. But one thing's for sure: it is hard for Moses to find a place there. Other biblical characters have passed through, or even been enshrined for a spell.

Elijah, for example. So close to Moses, almost the prophet's double, yet unquestionably a lesser figure. Why Elijah, then, rather than Moses? Because Elijah did not die, but was raised up to heaven in a whirlwind, on a chariot of fire, abandoning the mantle that had fallen from his shoulders to his disciple. Because Elijah will return, before the coming of 'the great and dreadful day', to 'turn the heart of the fathers to the children, and the heart of the children to their fathers' (Mal 4:5–6). Finally, perhaps, quite simply because Elijah was not as great as Moses and this actually enhances him in my eyes.

Readers may judge for themselves. After walking for forty days, Elijah, threatened with death by Queen Jezebel and deeply dispirited, reaches Horeb – another name for Mount Sinai – and takes refuge in a cave for the night. In the morning, the 'word of God' comes to him and requests him to go out and stand on the mountain. God reveals himself, just as he had to Moses centuries earlier on the same spot, but in a different and, above all, more ambiguous way: 'a great and strong wind rent the mountains, and brake in pieces the rocks before the Lord; but the Lord was not in the wind: and after the wind an earthquake; but the Lord was not in the earthquake: And after the earthquake a fire; but the Lord was not in the fire; and after the fire *a still small voice*' (I Kgs 19:11–12).[1] Elijah knew that God himself could be humble.

The prophet Elijah can speak to me, and I hear him. As I hear Esther, the Jewish Queen of Persia and Media, an ordinary woman who has the courage to hesitate and then the courage to act, who changes the course of fate and saves her people from a planned extermination, in the tale to which she has given her name and where that of God – astonishing paradox – does not appear once. Elijah still makes me dream and hope a little. I can even imagine running into him one day on a street corner, as in so many popular Jewish stories. Esther too inhabits a world that resembles mine: a disenchanted world this time, where God's name can no longer be uttered. But Moses? Immense, certainly, but brutal and remote as well. And definitely too kitsch.

Kitsch Moses

Obviously, we owe this kitsch very much to cinema. To Cecil B. DeMille, for example, and his *Ten Commandments*: seven months of filming, 10,000 extras, three hours and thirty-nine minutes of Technicolor.[2] But it's not only him.

We also owe it – if you'll forgive the irreverence – to Michelangelo. Even Freud does not manage to completely redeem his work when he makes out this stone Moses to be a Moses containing his anger and refusing to destroy the Tables*, and when he sees in 'the giant frame with its tremendous physical power' sculpted by the Italian simply 'a concrete expression of the highest mental achievement that is possible in a man, that of struggling successfully against an inward passion for the sake of a cause to which he has devoted himself'.[3] However 'mental' the 'achievement', it remains crushing. And the muscles are always there, in the stone, and not merely as a metaphor.

The kitsch is attributable in the first instance – if you'll forgive the blasphemy – to the Bible itself, which, even (or especially) when its language is ambiguous, always seems concerned to furnish us with garish scenes. For example, no one will ever be able to tell us for sure if the Moses who comes down the mountain transformed by his talks with God had a face that 'shone' or was wearing 'horns' (Exod 34:29).[4] Both possibilities have their defenders. They are sometimes combined, and we then find Moses's head emitting two rays . . . in the form of horns! This is all splendid, helping to fill (if needs be) a picture book which is already chock-full.

For the kitsch in Moses I am referring to is also due to this bric-a-brac of images. Images that are sometimes grandiose and often naive, enchanting the children we have remained but saddening the adults we have become, and which, willy-nilly, have ended up cluttering our memory and dominating our view for centuries. Here is something that ought to discourage my pen – I who have no desire, in the wake of so many others, to be the historian or analyst of a legacy which is rather too profuse, too glitzy, too rowdy.

Moses is certainly no second-rate hero, but this is not an argument in his favour. His mission, irrevocable and foundational, is imposing. He battles the despotic power of a megalomaniacal, pitiless pharaoh, and defeats him. He frees the Hebrews from slavery and provides them with a constitution, a Law dictated by God, which establishes them as a full-fledged nation and crowns their liberation. He severely punishes repeated instances of infidelity on the part of his flock, but also protects it from the excessive ire of the Almighty. For he is not afraid to oppose God himself, whose confidant he is and whom he sometimes induces to yield, bargaining for forgiveness and getting it (or less severe penalties, at least) for the recidivist rebels he is guiding through the desert. Moses leads Israel to the edge of the Promised Land, admittedly after various detours – forty years' wandering in the sands that permits embellishment of the saga with many a picturesque episode. Mission impossible, then, but mission accomplished. Or almost, because, despite everything, it falls to his successor, Joshua, to settle the Hebrews in their land by means of conquest. Even the prophet's death on the threshold of Canaan, far from diminishing his impressive stature, confirms and consecrates it. An exceptional Moses, certainly, but taking elegance to the point of not coming back to life at the story's end. Others have not shown such restraint. Conclusively mortal – and all the greater for it.

The Mosaic gesture is, as it should be, spectacular. Minor and major miracles succeed one another. Above all, major ones. The minor ones are pleasing, but little more. I shall therefore not expatiate on the rod turned into a snake and vice versa (Exod 4:2–4). And for good reason: the Egyptian magicians, with whom Moses must contend in a public contest to impress Pharaoh, have apparently mastered the technique pretty well themselves (Exod 7:11). And need we linger over another wonder, over the sign God generously vouchsafes to his prophet, over Moses's hand, which, when placed in his bosom, is covered with leprosy and then, placed there a second time, has its natural complexion restored (Exod 4:6–7)? Albeit temporary, this is a bit troubling surely? The Qur'an retains the episode while rewriting it: Moses's hand emerges from his lap 'white but unharmed' (28:32). Even though this whiteness has seemed wholly miraculous to some (in a man of presumably olive complexion), and given rise to esoteric interpretations, I do not see any particular reason to linger over it. So on to the major miracles! And there is no lack of them.

Thus we might, amazed, mention the bush that burns but is not consumed, from inside which God hails his prophet. Above all, seized with dread, let us enumerate the ten plagues that strike Egypt, but spare the Hebrews: the waters of the Nile turned to blood, frogs, lice, ravening beasts, dying livestock, ulcers, hail, locusts, darkness, death of the firstborn. Columns of fire and cloud guiding the people. Crossing of the Red Sea without getting wet, followed by the wholesale drowning of the enemy pursuers. Water gushing from rocks to slake the thirsty. Nourishing manna. Quails falling from the sky in the desert. The earth 'open[ing] her mouth, and swallow[ing]' the renegades, thus cast 'alive into the pit' (Num 16:32–3). Finally, and especially, the theophany on Sinai: thunder, lightning, trumpet blast, thick cloud, fire, smoke, the mountain trembling on its base. The catalogue of wonders is almost inexhaustible, and I shall not exhaust it here. At all events, one thing is clear: the divine Director did not skimp on resources. Others were subsequently able to profit from this. It is no accident if, in 1957, Cecil B. DeMille's biblical costume drama won a single Oscar: for special effects.

Perfect Moses

All this is grand. It is impressive. And the portrait of Moses the man – let us forget the hero with a divine mission for a moment – that emerges in the foreground of this formidable picture is commensurate with it. He is beautiful, 'of a beauty superior to that of an ordinary man', specifies Philo Judaeus.[5] A beauty, adds the Christian Gregory of Nyssa, to which he owed his life.[6] It dissuaded his birth parents from putting him to death and persuaded them to disobey Pharaoh's orders. It is what 'won' the heart of his adoptive mother, Pharaoh's daughter, when she found him drifting in his basket on the Nile. And if Moses is beautiful on the day of his birth (Exod 2:2), he remains so on the day of his death, which coincides with his 120th birthday: 'his eye was not dim, nor his natural force abated' (Deut 34:7).

Moses is therefore handsome, tall, and distinctly well-built. No one imagines a puny Moses. How could he play the role assigned to him? I shall not make much of his withstanding hunger and thirst. Even a weakling, provided he is sufficiently inspired by faith and has had a little training, will be able to go without bread and water – though not, perhaps, like Moses for forty days and forty nights in a row (Exod 34:28). No, this is not the kind of prowess, physical and spiritual, I have in mind, but something more trivial, more basic. The muscular strength that makes it possible, for example, for a man to descend a mountain laden with two heavy stone tablets on which God has engraved his Law; and then, in the rage provoked by discovery of the Golden Calf and the idolatrous worship his people have indulged in, to shatter these same tablets by casting them against the foot of that mountain. Anger and strength are conjoined in Moses, as they are in his God. This is the Moses glorified by Michelangelo, whatever else might have been said or written. And this is the Moses represented by Charlton Heston, as much athlete as actor.

A larger-than-life Moses: the Jewish tradition is as prone to this as others are. According to the Midrash, if the Bible takes care to inform us that the 'child' Moses 'grew' (Exod 2:10), when all children, by definition, grow, it is because he did not grow like everyone else. At the age of five, he was already an adult in intelligence, but also in size. Maybe intelligence would have been enough. But no, size had to be added to it. 'Powerful neck', 'broad shoulders', 'arms like two hammers' – thus, closer in time to us, is he seen by the Yiddish writer Sholem Asch (1880–1957).[7] Asch continues: 'Not a man strode here, but a giant who had fallen from heaven ... Everything about him was mighty, stature, limbs, and presence; everything about him was cut more sharply, with keener and straighter lines. . . . The sharp aquiline nose, the great circles of his eyes resting on their cushions and sending forth a commanding, heavenly light, the modelled features – these were dominant.'[8]

There are few biblical figures in the text of Scripture itself who are so present in the flesh as Moses: his body, his gaze, his hand, his arms are regularly referred to. As we have seen, posterity has not squandered the opportunity to magnify the physical presence of Moses to the point of caricature. The profile of the muscular prophet has one merit at least. It is at the antipodes of another, mocked and reviled yesterday, and still sometimes today, by anti-Semites and Zionists: that of the bowed, puny, pale Jew of Exile. One may welcome it like a breath of fresh air. But there is another side to the coin. For here we have something that also distances us from the possible humanity of Moses. A Moses larger than life, supernatural, (almost) divine. Here beauty and power are in fact simply the terrestrial and corporeal expression of a celestial, spiritual perfection. The life of the 'great' Moses, Gregory tells us, 'attained the extreme limit of perfection'; it can – and must – be described 'as a vivid model of beauty' and, by that token, offered for our imitation.[9] Before him, Philo had said much the same thing: 'like a well-fashioned painting', Moses 'presents himself and his life to our gaze, a work of utter beauty and divine form . . . a model for those who wish to imitate it'.[10]

Moses's perfection: a great prophet whose like would never be seen again (Deut 34:10). A prophet, but not only that. His panegyrists will not stop there. Moses possesses all the talents and excels in each of them. King, philosopher, legislator, high priest, and so forth. And even a general, which is not the least surprising! Granted, it is Moses who, shortly after the Exodus, ensures his troops victory over the Amalekites (Amalek). He does so simply by raising his arms to heaven, stationed on a hill, while Joshua conducts the actual battle below. When his arms are lowered, Israel falters. As soon as he raises them again, Israel regains the advantage. He will finally be aided by two deputies (his brother Aaron and Hur), who will support his arms when he begins to tire (Exod 17:8–13). When, later, Israel endeavours to attack Canaan contrary to God's express order, Moses 'departed not out of the camp' (Num 14:39–45). Scripture records the conquest of the northern part of Transjordan. Scarcely more. To discover a Moses who is genuinely a war leader, we need to look to extra-biblical traditions for help. Thus, Flavius Josephus* and various others place him at the head of a victorious campaign against Ethiopia, but this time on behalf of the Egyptians! His honour is thus safe: no string to Moses's bow is wanting. This man unquestionably did everything and did it better than anyone.

Tenacious Moses

Kitsch hero or perfect, quasi-divine being – does it matter, in the end? Should we not rather see these as two sides of a counterfeit coin? This way of overdoing things ill conceals an original deficit. At all events, it inevitably induces a desire in every cynic – that is, every reasonable person – to puncture the balloon. Others before me have tried, and not without some success. In his *Philosophical Dictionary* two and a half centuries ago, in the article on 'Moses', Voltaire soberly took stock in his inimitable fashion: (1) no source outside the Bible confirms the miracles attributed to Moses in the Pentateuch; (2) the Pentateuch could not have been written by Moses; (3) moreover, Moses probably never existed . . . The circle is complete, that's all there is to it. Exit Moses.

We may experience a temporary relief, but it will not last. For, however violent the historico-critical approach to Scripture invented in the West in the seventeeth century (a tradition that is probably much less 'violent' today than it was), it did not suffice to 'kill off' Moses, supposing this was what it had in mind. No, Moses is not dead. Ejected by the front door, he climbed back in through the window. If the historian's task is, among other things, to deconstruct the facts or, via a critique of sources, the traditionally received account, to say nothing of the proliferation of subsequent developments, this deconstruction of the facts and narrative never really impinges on the terrain of what obsesses us: the imaginary. At all events, it in no wise cancels its power. That machine never runs out of fuel and never stops working. It sometimes seems to generate monsters, which are rather frightening or ridiculous. But there is probably not much we can do about that.

Almost a century and a half after the publication of the *Philosophical Dictionary* Ahad Ha'am*, the inspirer of what has been called 'cultural' Zionism, seems to me to have answered Voltaire very powerfully on this score. In 1904 he published a long article simply entitled 'Moses'. In it he distinguished between two kinds of truth: 'archaeological' truth and 'historical' truth. In order to clearly understand what he meant, we must proceed to a transposition of terms. Ahad Ha'am's 'archaeological' truth is what we would call historical truth today: the truth that can be established by the critique of sources and the science of historians. The second – which he labelled 'historical' – is what we would call the truth of memory or the imaginary. In his view, the latter had nothing to fear from the former. Even if scholars proved beyond a shadow of a doubt that 'Moses the man' never existed, or was never as taught by Tradition, the 'ideal' Moses – 'our Moses', as he calls him – would remain the central figure in the Jewish collective imaginary, the ultimate embodiment of the expectations and spirit, in its generally unaccomplished purity, of a whole people.[11] A 'hero' is simply that, and the battering rams of science are ultimately unavailing against heroes, or pretty much so. For my part, I would add that the more tenuous the historical basis of the ideal hero, the less he has to fear from critical assault.

The 'ideal' Moses whose portrait is sketched by Ahad Ha'am in the remainder of his article – the figure said to permanently haunt the collective Jewish consciousness – is certainly not the multi-talented Moses we have already encountered. For starters, he is no longer a warrior. But nor is he a statesman, or even a legislator. He is fundamentally, exclusively, a prophet. And he is certainly not a priest – unlike his brother Aaron – since priests are the intermediate caste between the prophet and the world, transmitting, in an adaptive, circumstantial, contingent and degraded form, a 'prophetic ideal' that can 'influence [them] to a certain extent',[12] but little more. The prophet Moses is therefore a man of absolutes – absolute truth and absolute justice – incorrigibly recalcitrant to compromise. For that very reason, Moses must die. He must die so that the people may one day begin a normal life, its own life, beyond the Jordan. For its part, the prophet's spirit never dies. It continues secretly to animate the soul of the people that recognizes itself in it, even when appearing to betray it. As well as a fundamental meditation, Ahad Ha'am's article is also a piece of work dictated by the difficult historical moment Zionism was passing through in the early twentieth century, with the Ugandan project.[13] What the publicist was seeking to capture and define was the meaning, spirit and preconditions of an authentic Jewish leadership. But, however secularized the prophetic figure he constructed, a prophet for whom the voice of God is, in the first instance, an interior voice, his Moses impresses himself on us with as much force, power, stark exigency, and frightening beauty as the Moses of the Tradition, who once made us freeze or smile. In this respect, Ahad Ha'am utterly vanquished Voltaire. Tenacious and impregnable, Moses is ineluctably reborn (alas?) from his ashes.

So, is Moses never anything but implacable or risible – in a word: a monument? On one side, then, would be the French Romantic Alfred de Vigny, his famous poem of 1822 and his 'Moses' – 'very great', 'powerful and alone'. Or the Austrian Jewish composer Arnold Schoenberg*, his opera *Moses and Aaron*, begun in 1930, which remained unfinished, and his 'not at all human' prophet, the intransigent defender of an 'Idea' that he 'loves' more than his people, and which is the only thing he 'lives' for.[14] And on the other side, by way of a contrast that is perhaps only apparent, we have Superman – the Superman of the apologists or novelists – and even Superman in person, we might say. This will not have escaped readers. Like Moses saved from the hecatomb of Israel's male offspring ordered by Pharaoh, the comic-book character created by Joe Schuster and Jerry Siegel in the 1930s was rescued from the destruction of his native planet. The bulrush cradle of the first is replaced by the spacecraft that propels the second into space. Like Moses, Superman grows up as an adopted child and conceals his true identity from the outside world. And like Moses confronted with the Egyptian taskmasters, Superman realizes his vocation by reacting to the harsh realities of human injustice.

Is this really the only choice left to us? Surely not, which is what justifies writing this book. For there is another Moses, who could find his place, at least for a few pages, alongside Elijah and Esther in my uncertain, shifting Pantheon. A Moses who probably lends himself less to spectacular reconstructions; less to ideological recreations; and less to caricatures, too. A Moses who is very much present in the biblical tradition and the Jewish tradition, though more discreetly, more secretly, more intimately.

Meek Moses

For that tradition is itself distrustful of the heroic prophet whose image it has helped fashion. It is given to underscoring Moses's extreme modesty: 'Now the man Moses was very meek, above all the men which were upon the face of the earth' (Num 12:3). Only the angels, adds the Midrash, are gentler and humbler than he was. Moreover, this limit confirms the human character of Moses. Because he is a man, his modesty, extreme though it is, cannot be absolute. The Tradition is likewise happy to present the prophet as being as much the servant of God as the master of his people, if not more so. Thus, even today, when a believer

refers to Moses, and if she does so in Hebrew, it is the conse-
crated formula – 'Moses our Master' (*Mosheh Rabbenu*) – that
she spontaneously employs. God, however, refers to Moses first
and foremost as his servant: 'My servant Moses . . . who is faithful in all mine house' (Num 12:7). Certainly, the servant of a
king is, as a result of this proximity, like the king himself; and
what might seem to diminish Moses is, at the same time, what
enhances him. But, in the event, what counts is the absolute
ambivalence in Moses of smallness and grandeur. The prophet is
never greater than when small.

Similarly, he is never so divine as to cease to be human. When
he is going to die, and at the point where he blesses the children
of Israel, Moses is called *ish ha-Elohim*, 'man of God' (Deut
33:1). He is the only figure in the Pentateuch* to be referred to
thus, but not the only one in the Bible. Others after him will
enjoy this title – Elijah, for example, whom we are not upset to
find in such circumstances (I Kgs 17:18). It's true that in Exodus
Moses is directly called *elohim* ('god') twice. Yet Moses is only
relatively a 'god' in these instances. Just as Moses is the prophet
of God, his brother Aaron, Moses's spokesman, becomes
something like the prophet of Moses. And Moses becomes like
Aaron's god: 'And he [Aaron] shall be thy spokesman unto the
people: and he shall be . . . to thee a mouth, and thou shalt be to
him God' (Exod 4:16). Same thing when the ultimate recipient
of the divine message is not Israel, but Pharaoh: 'See, I have
made thee a god to Pharaoh; and Aaron thy brother shall be thy
prophet' (Exod 7:1). The deification of Moses? Strictly speaking,
no. Mere metaphor? Possibly more than that. The Jewish exegetical tradition closes the debate (provisionally) in these terms: for
Aaron, for Pharaoh, Moses was 'a master [*rav*]'.[15] Such is the
meaning of 'god' here: nothing more, nothing less.

The ambivalent status of Moses's character makes him an exception, since no man ever seems able to equal him, while holding him within the bounds of the rule: Moses is and remains a man. Nothing better attests to this than the fate reserved by the Bible and Tradition for Moses's body. The body of the prophet is not only the body magnified by so many artistic representations. This body is certainly exalted by Tradition. But from the outset the latter wounds it, too, and in the end expels it.

Dead Moses

I shall begin at the end. As a good exegetical method, this is not necessarily shocking and may also possess some heuristic virtue. The end, then: the death of Moses. Moses does not really die like everyone else. He to whom God speaks 'mouth to mouth' (*peh el-peh* in Hebrew) (Num 12:8) dies 'according to the mouth of the Lord' (*al pi ha-Shem*, which can also be translated as 'on the orders of the Everlasting God') (Deut 34:5). Rashi* construes this as Moses dying 'in a [divine] kiss'. This could simply mean that he died peacefully, without suffering. It might also mean – and this is different – that God himself came to gather his soul by kissing him on the mouth. At the time of his death, his body (as we already know) had not declined, had not aged. But Rashi goes much further: even after his death, his body's lifeblood did not leave it; its appearance did not alter; decomposition did not set in. In his tomb Moses reposes eternally fresh, as handsome as he was in his lifetime. And who buries him? Scripture does not specify, stating simply: 'he buried him in a valley' (Deut 34:6). There are two possibilities, according to Rashi: either Moses buried himself or God in person buried him.

The marvellous, the exceptional, the virtually non-human seem to dominate death here. Moses's death really is a beautiful death, a miraculous death. And yet, the evocation of it and the exegetic accretions around it remain ambiguous. At all events, Moses dies. And his body is interred. As such, his ultimate destiny is not fundamentally different from that of ordinary mortals. Despite the marvellous, the exceptional, his death is indeed a human death. For the scenario that obtains here involves rejection of a different possible scenario. For Flavius Josephus, for example, 'Moses was taken away from among men': 'A cloud stood over him on a sudden and he disappeared in a certain valley'.[16] Just like Elijah (as we have seen) and Enoch (Gen 5:24). The ancient rabbinical tradition registers this option: 'Some say that Moses is not dead, but continues to serve above.'[17] But this is evidently not the option of the compiler of the Bible, who takes an additional step.

While Moses himself is not 'taken away from among men', while his living body, escaping death, does not undergo any ascent into Heaven, his dead body, miraculously preserved as it is, disappears. 'And he buried him in a valley in the land of Moab, over against Beth-Peor: but no man knoweth of his sepulchre unto this day' (Deut 34:6). According to some, Moses himself did not know the site of his sepulchre. The prophet's tomb, according to Tradition, may well have been created, prepared, at the start of the history of the world, on the eve of the first Shabbat, 'at the confluence of day and night'.[18] But, 'unto this day', no one has been able to situate it. No Holy Sepulchre here. No possible profanation, nor any worship either. No one will ever go to mourn at Moses's graveside. No ascension for the body of Moses: simply a definitive eclipse. The fate of the prophet's body continues to be stamped by the seal of the exception. We are nevertheless liberated from it. The perfect body of the perfect prophet will never be held up for our contemplation.

In the end, then, Moses's body is expelled. This expulsion certainly further magnifies him. But it remains an expulsion. The extreme bodily presence of the living prophet is offset by the extreme bodily absence of the dead prophet. Making the dead prophet unlocatable is perhaps simply a way of restoring the living prophet to his rightful place. One exception cancels another. Exceptional when alive, exceptional when dead, Moses is finally normalized. Forever ambiguous.

Stammering Moses

In reality, Moses – the body of Moses – was ambiguous from the outset: wounded, imperfect, not up to the task. In this regard, one of the reasons with which Moses tries to justify refusing the mission God seeks to assign him merits our full attention. We may first of all record the initial arguments advanced by the prophet. First, he protests that he is unworthy: 'Who am I, that I should go unto Pharaoh, and that I should bring forth the children of Israel out of Egypt?' (Exod 3:11). God answers: 'I will be with thee' (Exod 3:12). He then queries the way that he will have to present the one who has sent him: 'and they shall say to me, What is his name? what shall I say unto them?' (Exod 3:13). God reveals to Moses his name: 'I AM THAT I AM' (Exod 3:14). Finally, he doubts whether he will win the support of the people: 'they will not believe me' (Exod 4:1). God empowers him to perform three miracles that will suffice to convince them.

Finally, as if in desperation, Moses invokes a strange impairment to get out of his mission. If I say 'strange', it is because the formulation of the scriptural text lacks precision: 'O my Lord, I am not eloquent, neither heretofore, nor since thou has spoken unto thy servant: but I am heavy of mouth, and of a heavy tongue' (Exod 4:10). To which God responds: 'I will be with thy mouth, and teach thee what thou shalt say' (Exod 4:12). The divine response is not enough for Moses: 'Please, O my Lord, make someone else thy agent' (Exod 4:13). It is then that God loses his temper, but agrees to give Moses a spokesman: his brother Aaron.

So, what is this impairment which compels Moses to persist in his refusal and obliges God to appoint Aaron alongside him? Which persuades him to duplicate the figure of Moses by that of Aaron? Which prompts him to, as it were, sever the body of the prophet in two, with he who hears (Moses) on one side and he who speaks (Aaron) on the other? Which leads him to recognize, establish and perhaps sanction a tension between the two that the sincerity of their collaboration will never cancel – a tension that reveals itself in all its disturbing intensity on the occasion of the Golden Calf? (Aaron cedes to the entreaties of the people and creates the Calf at their request, while Moses destroys the Calf and punishes the people for their idolatry.)

A temporary awkwardness of speech when Moses is thwarted or prey to an overly powerful emotion?[19] A problem of eloquence rather than elocution? Or less than that: a simple reticence on the part of Moses, reluctant to speak because 'in effect', 'when compared with that of God, human eloquence' is 'sheer speech-lessness'?[20] If Philo is to be believed, God ultimately has no difficulty reassuring him on this point: 'With my consent, everything will become articulate and correct, so that in the absence of any obstacle the stream of words will flow very easily and evenly from a pure source' – with Aaron serving at most as spokesman when it comes to making 'announcements to the people'.[21]

To borrow a formula from the Qur'an (20:27), it is certainly not easy to 'untie [Moses's] tongue'. This is a difficulty that has troubled more than one person. And Schoenberg, however brilliant his option, basically does little more than bypass it. From beginning to end of his opera, apart from one unique passage, Moses (bass) expresses himself in spoken-song (*Sprechgesang*), singing being reserved for his brother (tenor). Clearly, no opera, as no film or play, could ever represent a stammering prophet. Such a hero would elicit laughter rather than the sacred terror he is supposed to inspire. A medieval commentator, Rashbam*, grandson of Rashi, summarizes the terms of the problem very well: 'How could a prophet whom God has known face to face, and who received the Torah* from his hands, stutter?' So Moses's 'heavy tongue' must refer to something else – his poor command of the idiom in use in Pharaoh's palace, for example. Or his forgetting, after four decades' absence, of the Egyptian language. And yet Rashi himself is clear: 'I [Moses] speak clumsily [with heaviness]. And in the tongue of nations, [I am] *balbe*'. *Balbe* in Rashi's French, from the Latin *balbus*, simply means . . . 'stammerer' in our English. Here, we have an insistence that is endlessly intriguing.

An old rabbinical legend seeks after its fashion to clear up this curious mystery. Moses's elocution difficulties date back, it suggests, to an incident in his youth. One day, Pharaoh offered a banquet in the presence of his daughter and her adopted son. Moses, a toddler, an infant in the primary sense (that of the Latin *infans*, 'not yet speaking'), seized hold of Pharaoh's crown and placed it on his own head or, in a different version, threw it to the ground. In so doing, was he deliberately signalling, by virtue of his precocious intelligence, an ambition to destroy Pharaoh's power or even to supplant him on the Egyptian throne? The country's sages were assembled in all haste. Fortunately, the angel Gabriel, suitably disguised, slipped in among them. And he it was who proposed that the child should undergo a test. Let him be presented with a precious stone and a glowing coal on a tray. If, runs the legend, he grabs the first, he will be acting wisely and his earlier deed must therefore be taken seriously. Moses will then be put to death to remove the threat to Pharaoh's throne. If instead he grasps the burning coal, he is an infant without discernment, whose actions are devoid of significance, and he will be permitted to live. When the precious stone and the glowing coal are presented to Moses, he initially turns to the former. But the angel Gabriel invisibly guides his hand towards the coal, which he grabs and puts in his mouth, burning part of his lips and tongue. That is how, saved *in extremis* from certain death, Moses developed a speech impairment.

I can imagine the smile on my reader's face. This tale of an exceptionally gifted baby, precociously displaying his regal ambitions, and whom an angel must protect against his own intelligence; this story of the hot coal and the burnt hand, lips and tongue – should it not, along with various others, remain consigned to the kitschy hell on which I claimed to wish to shut the door for good? Perhaps. At least if we stick to this rather superficial reading. I think another reading is possible. The light of the wondrous should not induce illusions here. It does not quite dispel the eerie shadows. And the seeming naivety of the narrative may well conceal a genuine profundity.

There is in fact a dark side to this story, which underscores the inherent vulnerability of its hero. Moses is constantly in mortal jeopardy. He is imperilled on the day of his birth, when Pharaoh has just ordered all newborn Hebrew males to be cast into the Nile. He remains so three months later, when his biological mother, having hidden him, sets him adrift on the river. He is so once again when, having become an adult, he kills an Egyptian who is maltreating a Hebrew slave. Intent on imposing the capital penalty on Moses for this misdeed, Pharaoh forces him to flee. He is likewise threatened with death following the episode of the burning bush, when, returning to Egypt after having accepted the mission entrusted to him by God, a mysterious divine emissary seeks to kill him in the middle of the night.[22] And he will finally be so much later, when he asks God to exhibit his Glory to him: 'Thou canst not see my face: for there shall no man see me, and live' (Exod 33:20). The legend of the crown and the coal pertains precisely to this logic. It places Moses in mortal danger at the royal court, when he has just been taken in by Pharaoh's daughter – a danger he escapes only at the last minute through the intervention of the heavenly messenger. But there is more. The character's fundamental vulnerability is definitively stamped on Moses's body by the legend: in the burnt lips and tongue. Moses's body is wounded, marked with a foundational impairment, which may well save him from death, but decisively affects (so it would appear) his ability to carry out the mission assigned him by God on his own and in full. This does not prevent God from choosing the impaired man for his prophet, or sticking with his choice when the prophet invokes his infirmity to query it. Has God suddenly untied Moses's tongue? We may doubt it. Some traditions say that while he could have made a new man of him, he refrained from doing so. Why, moreover, if he had miraculously cured his stammering prophet, would he have appointed Aaron to speak in his place?

Uncircumcised Moses

In truth, in the biblical text, Moses himself uses another expression to signal his handicap. Once again hesitating to carry God's word to Israel's oppressor, he exclaims: 'Behold, I am of uncircumcised lips [*aral sefatayim*], and how shall Pharaoh hearken unto me?' (Exod 6:30). Here we are no longer dealing with mere 'heaviness' of the mouth, but non-circumcision. The term is at once more precise, more evocative and more mysterious.

No less so than heaviness, this non-circumcision is certainly metaphorical. However, the metaphor could have been more abstract, if I may put it like that, and Moses might simply have declared himself 'of uncircumcised speech'. Instead, as with heaviness, but symbolically even more laden with significance, this uncircumcised state is clearly associated with a physical organ of Moses's body: his lips. His difficulty in speaking, the Bible stresses, just as it was stressed by the legend, is physically inscribed on Moses's body. And indicated by a word that is anything but neutral.

Moses uncircumcised is not exactly insignificant, even metaphorically, and even if it is only his lips. In the Hebrew and Jewish context, not to be circumcised is an unequivocal impairment. The uncircumcised body might seem whole, but it is not. It is circumcision – an ablation – that renders the body perfect. Contrary to appearances, it is circumcision that realizes the integrity of the male body, which is thus not given but acquired. Only the circumcised male body is whole. And any non-circumcision – even of the metaphorical variety – means imperfection.

Thus, one may have an uncircumcised heart, closed to the truth (Deut 10:16). One may have an uncircumcised ear, deaf to the word of God (Jer 6:10). Finally, one may have uncircumcised lips, like Moses. And this non-circumcision of the lips, whether inborn or the effect of a childhood injury, is indeed an impairment in Moses, a reminder of his vulnerability and mortality. It re-humanizes the prophet's body, it re-humanizes the prophet himself, by signalling and highlighting his irreme-diable imperfection.

Moses only ever just escapes perfection. As he only just escapes death. A curious silence in the biblical account of his birth and early infancy is bound to attract our attention in this respect. Nothing is said there about circumcision. I am speaking this time, obviously, of circumcision in the literal sense: the ablation of the foreskin to which every newborn Hebrew male is subjected. A comparison between this account and that of another birth, no less foundational than Moses's – that of the patriarch Isaac, son of Abraham and Sarah – clearly brings out the relative strangeness: 'Sarah conceived, and bare Abraham a son . . . Abraham called the name of his son that was born unto him . . . Isaac. And Abraham circumcised his son Isaac being eight days old, as God had commanded him' (Gen 21:2–4). Nothing of the sort is mentioned in Moses's case: not a word about his father; nothing on the name given him at birth by his parents; above all, not a word about his circumcision.

Such silence cannot but echo strangely in the ear of a Jewish reader. A rabbinical teaching endeavours to 'normalize' the account by filling in the gaps: 'Moses's parents saw the child and his appearance resembled that of an angel of God. They circum-cised him on the eighth day.'[23] However angelic the appearance of this very beautiful baby, it is therefore a baby like any other: a male, it was born imperfect – duly equipped with a foreskin – and, like every ordinary male baby, has been subject to the dual ceremonial of naming[24] and circumcision.

Unless we should interpret that curious silence quite differ-ently; unless there is, in fact, no gap to fill. If the biblical text says nothing about Moses's circumcision, perhaps it is for a very simple reason: he was not circumcised. Because he was born ready-circumcised, already the bearer of the sign of the Covenant* – in a word, perfect, and hence no ritual act prescribed by the Law is required to perfect him: 'What could his mother see in him that made him more beautiful and better than any man? Simply that he was born circumcised.'[25]

In such a context, the non-circumcision of Moses's lips seems more than ever welcome. It makes it possible for us to accommodate the male member that appeared unimpaired the day he came into the world. For what now counts, saving Moses at the last minute, but radically and definitively, from a perfection liable to distance him from us forever, is that he is damaged – whether from birth or following some childhood accident – in the very organ associated with prophecy: his tongue, his lips, his mouth. However great, however incomparably great, this prophet has a stammer. If he is, perhaps, only greater as a result, he is also diminished. The infirmity is certainly surmounted, but it is not abolished and it affects the most essential thing. Moses needs Aaron. However great he is, he is not self-sufficient. He is a being of paradox. Like every human being.

Pure is the truth that Moses reveals to us and perfect the Torah that God gave him the mission of transmitting. Nevertheless, this Torah was in the first instance stammered out by a stammering prophet.

2

The Egyptian Woman's Son

Moses: the name is so familiar to us that we do not spontaneously ponder its origin or meaning. An adjective has been derived
from it – 'Mosaic', 'relating to the prophet or his doctrine';[1] and
even the name of an object, 'moïse' in French, 'Moses basket' in
English ('small portable cot made of wickerwork'). All this
remains rather exotic, and infrequent, but nevertheless involves a
form of linguistic acclimatization that helps neutralize the very
real strangeness of the prophet's name.

The banality of Moses, an all-purpose word, a noun that can
be used to say anything. A bid to protect Venice against the
ravages of the sea? 'Project Moses'. Israel's airlift of several
thousand Falasha from Ethiopia in 1984–85? 'Operation Moses'.
Fine. But what does Moses mean? And where does it come from?
Of whom – of what – is Moses the name? The answer lies in a
single verse of Exodus. But on this issue, as on others, the
answer, which is only apparently of 'biblical simplicity', sounds
like another question.

No One, Son of No One

It is Pharaoh's daughter who, having saved the infant from the water of the Nile and adopted him, names him: 'she called his name Moses [*Mosheh*]: and she said, Because I drew him [*meshi-ti-hu*] out of the water' (Exod 2:10). This account, reminiscent of others, tends to enrol Moses in the patriarchal epic. The prophet thus derives his name from a play on words and the circumstances of his rescue, just as others before him, ancestors of the Hebrews, derived their name from a play on words and the circumstances of their conception or birth. Abraham called his son Isaac, *Yitzhak* ('he will laugh'), because his mother Sarah, who was ninety, 'laughed' when she was told that she had conceived and would give birth at such an advanced age (Gen 18:12); and because God, in keeping his promise, had made her a subject of 'laughter' and an occasion for rejoicing (Gen 21:6). Isaac himself called his youngest son Jacob (*Ya'akov*), because when he emerged from his mother's womb he was holding the heel (*akev*) of his twin Esau (Gen 25:26). The examples are legion and so, if we do not look too closely, Moses doesn't really stand out.

But only if we do not look too closely; only if we regard wordplays as inconsequential games.

Because this is far from being the case. A man's name, in good biblical tradition, always tells us something of what he is. The name is the sign and inception of a destiny or vocation. The best proof of this is that any major alteration in the trajectory of an individual can, and sometimes even must, translate into a change of name. When God seals his covenant with him, Abram becomes Abra*h*am and Saraï becomes Sara*h*, the addition of *he* to their name signalling the universalization of their status: Abraham becomes a father to all humanity and Sarah a princess for all nations.[2] After having struggled with the Angel, Jacob becomes Israel, because he has 'vanquished' God. Given the major importance of the character, Moses's name does not, and obviously cannot, diverge from this rule. Like the circumstances of its choosing, the name necessarily says something essential about the man.

Up to this point, if I may put it thus, everything is in order: Moses does not seem any different from his predecessors. But to this point only. For as soon as we take a rather closer look, everything begins to get complicated. Moses does not derive his name from his father, his mother, or God, but from a foreign woman: an Egyptian. The name is not given to him at birth, or even on the day of his rescue (occurring three months later), but only when, the child having 'grown', he is presented by his nurse to Pharaoh's daughter (Exod 2:10). For several months, then, and probably much longer, Moses remains nameless. Worse, if we stick to the highly economical terms of the account in Exodus 2, Moses is the child of two families – his birth family and his adoptive family – none of whose members is named themselves. We know only that his biological father and mother are of the tribe of Levi and that he has a sister. For her part, his adoptive mother likewise remains anonymous: she is simply 'Pharaoh's daughter'. For several months, then, and probably longer, Moses's true name is No One, Son of No One. His very birth is strikingly ordinary: 'And there went a man of the house of Levi, and took to wife a daughter of Levi. And the woman conceived, and bare a son' (Exod 2:1–2). Here, we have no complicated story of sterility miraculously overcome, of the kind the patriarchal epic abounds in. Even the threat hanging over the baby is insufficient to distinguish him: it hangs over all the male infants of the Hebrews. His mother finds him 'goodly', certainly, but what mother doesn't find her offspring beautiful? We must wait a while for the destiny of the infant to assume a genuinely distinctive tonality, with his consignment to the Nile and his rescue by the daughter of a foreign king – the very king who, in principle, wishes him dead. It changes above all when, very belatedly, 'Pharaoh's daughter' finally names him. It is at this precise moment – and at Pharaoh's court – that there begins, strictly speaking or properly named, the life of Moses: an Egyptian Moses, the (adoptive) son of an Egyptian woman, from whom he has received his name.

The Holy Family

All this is obviously awkward for a certain rabbinical tradition. Can Moses the Egyptian, Moses the late-named, accede without further ado to the unique status he has in the history of Israel and Revelation? Happily, the account in Exodus 2 supplies some welcome correctives to this disturbing picture. The Hebrew mother does indeed abandon her son, but not completely, since she entrusts his safekeeping to her daughter, who 'stood afar off' from the river's waters 'to wit what would be done to him' (Exod 2:4). Next, Pharaoh's daughter clearly recognizes him for what he is: 'This is one of the Hebrews' children', she says seeing him floating on the Nile in his wicker basket (Exod 2:6). Finally, it is his Hebrew mother who suckles the new-born and she it is whom Pharaoh's daughter takes on as a nurse, on his sister's advice, and (so it would seem) unaware of the tie that binds her to the nursling.

Moses the Egyptian therefore enjoys a Hebrew early infancy, one free, as it were, of foreign taint. The breastfeeding makes up for the abandonment. The milk bond duplicates the blood tie, a tie shortly to be strengthened as the Exodus narrative continues.

Once she has given Moses a name, 'Pharaoh's daughter', a problematic adoptive mother, completely disappears from the plot. By contrast, Aaron, Moses's brother, shows up and becomes the prophet's deputy (Exod 4:14). The names of their parents – Amram and Jochebed – soon emerge in a genealogy of the descendants of Levi (Exod 6:20). And their sister reappears in her turn, under the name of Miriam and in the guise of a prophetess, singing the miracle of the crossing of the Red Sea (Exod 15:20). At last! The (holy) family is thoroughly in order; it has found its bearings and its names. Genealogy has reasserted its prerogatives.

However, these biblical correctives would not be enough for the rabbinical tradition, which did its utmost to reshape the story of Moses's birth and early infancy into a typically patriarchal narrative logic – one, moreover, saturated with the supernatural – and to erase any suspicion of compromise with the emblematic, despised, idolatrous power: Egypt. This, according to tradition, is what really happened:

Amram was one of the great men of his generation, a spiritual leader of the Hebrews in Egypt, a senior patriarchal figure. Registering Pharaoh's decree, which doomed all the newborn males of Israel to a certain death by drowning, he decided to renounce procreation and divorced his wife, Jochebed. All the Hebrews emulated him. Miriam then intervened with her father, criticizing him: (1) for thereby condemning more children to oblivion than had Pharaoh himself, since not to procreate was also to condemn girls; (2) for depriving these unconceived children of existence not only in this world (as had Pharaoh), but also in the world to come; and (3) for forgetting that the decree of a sinful man like the ruler of

Egypt might very well not be fulfilled, whereas his – that of a righteous man – definitely would be. Persuaded by his daughter's arguments, Amram retracted his decision and took his wife again for new nuptials. And all the Hebrews did the same.[3]

When Amram remarried Jochebed, she was 130 (forty years older than Sarah when she gave birth to Isaac). Miraculously, she recovered her youth and gave birth to Moses. When he came into the world, Moses filled the house with light. That is why his mother found him 'beautiful' or 'goodly' (*tov*), just as God found the light 'good' when he created it (Gen 1:4). This divine light would never leave the newborn. When Pharaoh's daughter opened the wicker basket she had fished out of the waters of the Nile, what did she see? The child and, beside him, the divine Presence. Why did she employ a wet nurse from among the Hebrews? Because the child had refused to suckle the breast of the Egyptian nurses presented to him: he could not soil the mouth with which he knew he was destined to speak with the divine Presence. And Pharaoh's daughter might well have been vaguely aware that the woman she entrusted the infant to was the same who had borne him.[4]

The scriptural account unfolded a simple plot, free of marvels, almost ordinary, in which God does not directly intervene at any point. Its rabbinical rewrite does quite the opposite, which clearly possesses more than one advantage. Moses is no longer the beautiful nursling, child of an anonymous couple, who has come into the world just like everyone else, and whom his mother initially tries to conceal in order to save him, only finally – when she cannot hide him any longer – to abandon him to the Nile in the hope that some kind hand will come to his aid. Baby Moses has definitely gone up in status. He is now part of an impeccable genealogy. He is no longer born to an anonymous father, but to a grandee of Israel. And it is not only his rescue that is miraculous, but his very birth. Moses is born to a doubly sterile couple. Sterile in the first instance because separated, in line with the father's decision; and then because of the mother's very great age. From his advent, a supernatural light marks Moses out as an uncommon being. From his advent he maintains an astonishing familiarity with the divine Presence. And he is already sufficiently conscious of the extraordinary destiny that will be his to refuse any impure contact, including the breast of an Egyptian wet nurse. Egypt washes over him without touching him. And even the Egyptian woman who rescued him must ultimately return him to his own and disappear.

Naming Moses

Everything therefore turns out for the best. Or almost. Because there still remains one insurmountable difficulty: Moses's name. The one by which we know him; by which God himself knows him; and the only one by which he is referred to throughout the Torah. The name he was given, it would seem, by none other than that Egyptian woman. Did she know Hebrew, since the name she chose for the infant – *Mosheh* – makes sense in Hebrew and seems to be based on a Hebraic root – *M-Sh-H* – which evokes the act of 'removing' from the waters, rather as one 'removes' a hair from a bowl of milk? That said, in Hebrew at least, *Mosheh* emphatically does not mean 'Removed' (from the waters), but 'Remover'. In other words, Moses in Hebrew is not 'he who is removed' (from the waters), but 'he who removes'. Maybe the Egyptian woman did not know Hebrew as well as all that. Hard to say. Perhaps she mastered it better than anyone. Most importantly, she knew that a name is not only the trace of a past deed. It is also, and above all, the announcement of a destiny. That is doubtless why more than one biblical name is in the future (or the imperfect). Isaac, *Yitzhak*, is not he who laughed, but he who will laugh. Jacob, *Ya'akov*, is not he who came hot on another's heels, but he who will do so. And Israel, *Yisra'el*, is not he who vanquished God, but he who will do so. Why, then, should Moses not be 'he who removes' (or will remove) after being 'he who was removed'? Is this not confirmed by the story's sequel? Is it not Moses who led out, delivered, 'removed' the Hebrews from slavery? And is it not he who saved them, delivered them, 'removed' them from the waters of the Red Sea? Not such a bad Hebraist, then, this Egyptian woman. She chose the name very aptly. And she thereby manifested something akin to prophetic skill. She saw that Moses's past prefigured his future and that what he had benefited from as a passive infant would be employed by him as an active adult for the benefit of a whole people. Yesterday the object of a passive 'removal', he would be the subject, tomorrow, of an active one.

Nevertheless, can this role of 'naming prophetess', who in naming heralds the singular destiny of the named, be so readily granted to Pharaoh's daughter? Is it possible or admissible to confer on her more than the status of part-time, adoptive mother and unconscious tool in the hands of Providence for saving Israel's future saviour? This difficulty – this trap – is hardly negligible, for what is at stake is nothing less than the identity of Moses: an identity from which it is imperative to exclude any suspicion of 'Egyptianness'. The rabbinical tradition would hit upon three alternative ways of ensuring this. By arguing that it was not Pharaoh's daughter who gave Moses his name; by arguing that at the time she named him, Pharaoh's daughter was not, or no longer, Egyptian; or by arguing that 'Moses' was not, in reality, the only name given to the prophet. Let us examine these alternatives one by one.

First option: it was not Pharaoh's daughter who gave Moses his name. This option is not perhaps the most convincing. However, it has the advantage of purely and simply eliminating the inconvenient character. It is based on a reinterpretation/ redraft of Exodus 2:10: 'And the child grew, and she brought him unto Pharaoh's daughter, and he became her son. And she called his name Moses: and she said, Because I drew him out of the water.' This verse contains three characters. One male character: the child, who grows, who is brought, who is adopted, and who is finally named. And two female characters: the natural mother (who is also the wet nurse) and the adoptive mother, Pharaoh's daughter. Four actions are attributed to a female character: the infant's presentation, adoption and naming, and the interpretation of the name given him. There is no dispute about the first two: it is indeed the biological mother who brings the infant to Pharaoh's daughter and it is the latter who makes him her adoptive son. Likewise with the fourth action: only Pharaoh's daughter can evoke the rescue of Moses as she does, in the first person. There remains the third, most crucial action: the naming. 'And she called his name Moses'. Who is 'she'? Are we absolutely certain that it is still Pharaoh's daughter? That 'she' is anonymous and ambiguous. And what if it were Moses's biological mother, Jochebed, who would thereby become the only genuine 'naming prophetess' – a Hebrew! – in the story? Indeed, why not rewrite our verse thus: 'And the child grew, and [his natural mother Jochebed] brought him unto Pharaoh's daughter, and he became [Pharaoh's daughter's] son. And [Jochebed] called his name Moses: and [once Jochebed had explained to her the meaning of the Hebrew term, Pharaoh's daughter, finding it highly appropriate] said, Because I drew him out of the water'?[5]

Second option: when she names Moses, Pharaoh's daughter is not – or is no longer – an Egyptian. In fact, she figures among the biblical characters whom the rabbinical tradition makes proselytes, whether Scripture explicitly lends itself to this or not. In rescuing Moses from the fate Pharaoh had decreed for him, as for all his cohort, she commits an act of rebellion against her own father. In adopting the infant whom she has saved, she extends and crowns a process of conversion that is, in the first instance, a recantation of idolatry. Rupture with the earthly father, adherence to the celestial Father, the conversion of Pharaoh's daughter is, like all conversions, accompanied by a renaming. She will henceforth be called Bithiah, or *Bat-Yah*, 'daughter of God'. Emergence from anonymity and escape from idolatry thus coincide in a new genealogical inscription. The name bestowed on her is a Hebrew name, and it is bestowed by God: 'The Holy One, blessed be his name, said to Bithiah, Pharaoh's daughter (*bat Par'o*): "Moses was not your son, and you called him your son; just so you, who are not my daughter (*biti*), I shall call my daughter (*biti*)".'[6] Renamed by God himself, Bithiah, who strictly speaking is no longer Pharaoh's daughter, can quite legitimately name the budding prophet. She even affords him, symbolically, a most valuable genealogical supplement. Moses is no longer simply the son of Amram and Jochebed, of the tribe of Levi. As the (adoptive) son of Bithiah, herself the (adoptive) daughter of God, he becomes, so to speak, the (adoptive) grandson of God. The Egyptian woman, by ceasing to be such and thus erecting an extra barrier between Moses and Egypt, far from threatening the prophet's Hebrew identity, confirms it, settles it, and even enhances it with divine kinship.

Third option: 'Moses' was not in fact the only name given to the prophet. The Midrashic tradition is not reconciled to the unicity of Moses's name. Nor does it accept that he could have remained unnamed until Pharaoh's daughter intervened. The same account, cited above,[7] which could not let Moses labour under the least suspicion of not having been circumcised, can scarcely envisage his natural parents not giving him a name at birth: 'Moses's parents saw the child and his appearance resembled that of an angel of God. They circumcised him on the eighth day and named him Yekutiel.'[8] Elsewhere, there are six names, or designations, generously accorded to Moses. He is also called (1) Yered, because he 'caused to descend' (*horid*) the Torah; (2) the 'father of Gedor', or the father or first of the saviours (*godrin*) of Israel; (3) Heber, because he 'linked' (*hiber*) the sons to their Father who is in Heaven; (4) 'the father of Sokho', or the father and first of the prophets who 'see' (*sokhim*) the Spirit of Holiness; (5) Yekutiel, because he brought the sons to hope (*mekavin*) in their father who is in Heaven; and, finally, (6) 'the father of Zanoah', the father and the first of those who brought about renunciation (*maznihim*) of idol worship in Israel.

This third option – which is, as we shall see, closely associated with the second – in no wise cancels the absolute privilege, the uncontested pre-eminence, of the name 'Moses'. Nor does it dissolve the privileged link between the prophet and the first to name him, but actually reinforces it. It is precisely in the context of the Midrashic elaboration around the name and character of Bithiah[9] that these six alternative designations of the prophet appear. It concludes with these words, of total clarity: 'The Holy One, blessed be his name, said to Moses: "By your life, out of all the names you have been called by, to refer to you I use the only name by which Bithiah, Pharaoh's daughter, called you.'" These six alternative designations are ultimately no less associated with Bithiah, Pharaoh's daughter, than with Moses's natural mother. The Midrash did not invent them. It found them in a mysterious verse in the Book of Chronicles: 'And his wife Yehudijah bare Yered the father of Gedor, and Heber the father of Sokho, and Jekutiel the father of Zanoah. And these are the sons of Bithiah the daughter of Pharaoh' (I Chr 4:18). The proposed exegesis is crystal-clear: there are only three characters here. 'Yered the father of Gedor, and Heber the father of Sokho, and Jekutiel the father of Zanoah' are one and the same man, as we already know: Moses. He is surrounded by two maternal figures: 'his wife, Yehudijah' (the Judean or Jewess) is obviously Jochebed – the natural mother who gave birth to him; while 'Bithiah the daughter of Pharaoh' is someone we are already familiar with – the adoptive mother, of whom Moses is (albeit in a different way) 'the son'. Another exegesis goes much further. In reality, Jochebed is completely absent from this verse and one mother, one only, is mentioned there twice: Bithiah. 'Yehudijah' is her. So, is this Egyptian woman 'Judean' (or Jewish)? Definitely, once she no longer worships her idols and has converted to the one true faith.[10] But can it really be said that she gave birth to Moses? And can he really be held to be her 'son'? Certainly, once she has provided for his education. To instruct a child, even someone else's child, is to make him one's son.[11]

The three options we have examined pursue a single goal: to ensure that the naming of Moses owes nothing to Egypt, thus erasing any hint of Egyptianness in Moses himself. Option 1 – the least interesting – totally excludes the adoptive mother in favour of the birth mother: it is Jochebed who names Moses, not

Pharaoh's daughter. Options 2 and 3 employ the converse strategy. 'Pharaoh's daughter' remains the focus, to the extent of eclipsing Jochebed. But she ceases to be 'Pharaoh's daughter' and becomes Bithiah, 'daughter of God', and the Egyptian in her gives way to the 'Jewess'. Moses still has two mothers, but both are now 'Jewish': Jochebed, the mother who is Jewish by blood, and Bithiah, the mother who is Jewish in spirit. And it might even be said that he has two fathers: Amram, Moses's father by blood, and God himself, the father of Bithiah in spirit, who is Moses's mother in spirit.

Moses and the Egyptian Man

But we cannot stop there. No exegetical throw of the dice, however successful, will ever abolish the persistent chance of the texts. This fine portrait of a woman, Egyptian by birth and Jewish by choice, looks like a decidedly fragile artifice. After all, how can it stand up against an account – the biblical one – that perseveres in highlighting the ambiguity of Moses's identity?

On reaching adulthood, Moses returns to 'his brethren' and 'looks on their burdens' (Ex 2:11). Rashi stresses: 'He applies his eyes and his heart to suffering for them.' Obviously, this suggests some effort. As if Moses's compassion for his brothers were not automatic, did not spontaneously well up in him. Moreover, is it the suffering of his own kind that outrages him? Is it not rather the sight of injustice that scandalizes him? Certainly, when he sees 'an Egyptian man' [*ish mitzri*] beating 'a Hebrew, one of his brethren', he stands up for the latter, strikes the former, kills him and hides his body in the sand. So, is this Moses the Hebrew coming to the aid of his Hebrew brothers? Not necessarily. The following day, he tries to intervene with two Hebrews who are quarrelling. He says to the instigator: 'Wherefore smitest thou

thy fellow?' (Exod 2:13). What shocks him here? The fact that
two Hebrews are fighting, rather than behaving like brothers? Or
simply the injustice done to the 'fellow', the other man? Forced
to flee Egypt when the news of his murder reaches Pharaoh,
Moses enters the country of Midian. And what does he find
there? Some shepherds maltreating seven young women at the
well where they have come to water the flock of their father
Jethro, the local priest. Once again, Moses intervenes and chases
off the violent shepherds. This time, the dispute is not between
Hebrew and non-Hebrew, or between Hebrew and Hebrew, but
between non-Hebrews (Midianites). So, Moses the Jew born-and-
bred concerned for the fate of his brethren? Or a righteous man
eager for justice between human beings? Having returned home
with their flock, Jethro's daughters will not bother with such
subtleties, recounting their fortunate escape to their father thus:
'An Egyptian man [*ish mitzri*] delivered us out of the hand of the
shepherds, and also drew water enough for us, and watered the
flock' (Exod 2:19). Moses 'an Egyptian man'? This is intriguing.
Persistent textual chance! At the very moment he flees Egypt
because he is in mortal danger for having killed 'an Egyptian
man', Moses is himself perceived as 'an Egyptian man' by the
Midianite women whom he has just rescued. It is as if he ineluctably remained the son of the Egyptian woman.

In these circumstances, as in others, appearances turn out to
be misleading. Yet it all started so well. The scene of the fleeing
Hebrew arriving in a foreign land, sitting down at the edge of a
well, and seeing the seven daughters of Jethro come to water
their father's sheep, was in the best of taste. This touching scene
summons up other, older ones, which were no less touching.
That, for example, of the servant sent by Abraham to Chaldea to
find a wife for his son: once arrived, the servant has his camels

kneel down near a fountain at evening, around the time the women come to draw water, and decides that the one who agrees to quench his thirst and water his camels will be Isaac's intended. Rebekah is the one (Gen 24:10–27). And that other scene where now it is Jacob who, arriving in Haran, rolls the stone from the rim of the well where he has stopped and waters Laban's sheep, led there by his daughter Rachel, whom Jacob falls for and marries after various misadventures (Gen 29:2–11). The episode where Moses rescues Jethro's daughters from the Midianite shepherds and waters their flock is, then, delightfully patriarchal and authentically Hebrew. Moreover, according to the Midrash, as Rashi stresses, it is precisely in the hope of finding a wife that the fugitive sits down where he does: 'He has learned [from the experience] of Jacob, who found a wife at the well.' And this is precisely what happens: Moses meets his future wife – Zipporah, daughter of Jethro.

Yet the echoes are only partial. It was to his 'country', his 'native land', that Abraham sent his servant to seek a spouse for his son; and the person he brought back – Rebekah – was a close relative of the patriarch (his great-niece, in fact). Similarly, it was in Haran, the city his family hailed from, that Jacob met Rachel, 'the daughter of Laban his mother's brother' (Gen 29:10) – in a word, his cousin. Nothing of the sort in Moses's case. Midian means nothing to him. It is neither Egypt nor the native land of his Hebrew forebears. The woman he weds is a foreigner and, what's more, the daughter of a local idolatrous priest. The rabbinical tradition seeks to dismiss this problem by arguing that Jethro 'had left idolatry behind' and had, as a result, been 'banished' from Midian and forced to settle in the desert.[12] But it goes even further when commenting on a subsequent episode. The Bible recounts that, having heard of the extraordinary way in which God had delivered the Hebrews from Egypt, Jethro came to join Moses accompanied by Zipporah and the two children she had borne the prophet (Exod 18). And the rabbis specify that Jethro presented himself thus to his son-in-law with a view to converting to Judaism.[13] However, the naturalization and Judaization of Moses's in-laws do not suffice to alleviate the disastrous effects of a stubborn fact: the prophet had not a second's hesitation in marrying a foreign woman, in a foreign land, and having children with her.[14] The rabbinical tradition itself does not speak with one voice on this delicate subject. It recalls that Moses went so far as to enter into a strange agreement with his idolatrous father-in-law to win the hand of his daughter. According to its terms, the first child to be born from his union with Zipporah would be raised as a Gentile and given over to idol worship; only the next would be raised as Hebrews and devoted to the service of the Everlasting God.[15]

At all events, even if we put aside possible uncertainties as to the actual religious identity – idolatrous or Judaic – of Moses's in-laws, and even if we regard the disturbing tale of the pact with Jethro as baseless gossip, two words of scriptural text suffice to shatter irreparably the reassuring image of the traveller who, like other Hebrews before him, meets his future wife at the well. As we have seen, these two words are uttered by the daughters of Jethro: *ish mitzri*. For them, no doubt about it: it was an 'Egyptian man' who rescued them from the shepherds' violence.

Naturally, the rabbinical tradition does not fail to react in the usual way: 'Moses, an Egyptian? He was dressed as an Egyptian, yes, but he was a Hebrew!'[16] Clothing is not quite enough to make one an Egyptian. Only the daughters of Jethro could be fooled by the get-up of a traveller who had left his country in a hurry, without even time to change. It's odd, even so, that Moses did not take the trouble to set things straight. To state, as we would say today, his true identity.

Unless, adds the same source, Moses actually related his adventures to Jethro's daughters and we should construe what they said to their father as follows: '[His killing of] an Egyptian man [forcing him to flee, led Moses here, and he] rescued us from the shepherds . . .' This sleight of hand recalls another: Jochebed replacing Pharaoh's daughter in the role of namer of her infant. It might seem ingenious. In truth, however, the remedy is worse than the illness.

Let us go back to the beginning. We read 'an Egyptian man' and, since it manifestly seemed to refer to the saviour and protector of Jethro's daughters, we regarded it as a description – somewhat troubling, to be sure, but clear – of Moses. But now we have this Midrashic elaboration that implicitly discloses another character behind Moses: the 'Egyptian man' whom Moses killed because he was mistreating a Hebrew. Given that the effect of the second reading cannot at a stroke magically erase the effect of the first, the second character does not completely supplant the first. The figure of the Righteous man is no sooner erased than that of the Evil one is superimposed on it.

Might they have something in common?

Moses, Jesus and the Blasphemer

The phrase 'Egyptian man' appears three times, and three times only, in the story of Moses as recounted in the Pentateuch. The first time it refers to the Egyptian killed by Moses (Exod 2:11). The second time, as we have just seen, it refers to Moses himself (or possibly, once again, to the Egyptian killed by Moses) (Exod 2:19). Finally, on the third occasion it refers to the father of a blasphemer whom Moses has stoned by the community of Israel as a punishment for his crime many years later, during an episode in the trek through the desert narrated in Leviticus (Lev 24:10–23):

> And the son of an Israelitish woman, whose father was an Egyptian man, went out among the children of Israel. And this son of the Israelitish woman and a man of Israel strove together in the camp. And the Israelitish woman's son blasphemed the name of the Lord, and cursed. And they brought him unto Moses. (And his mother's name was Shelomith, the daughter of Dibri, of the tribe of Dan). And they put him in ward, that the mind of the Lord might be shewed them. And the Lord spake unto Moses, saying, Bring forth him that hath cursed without the camp; and let all that heard him lay their hands upon his head, and let all the congregation stone him. . . . And he that blasphemeth the name of the Lord, he shall surely be put to death, and all the congregation shall certainly stone him: as well the stranger, as he that is born in the land, when he blasphemeth the name of the Lord, shall be put to death. . . . And Moses spake to the children of Israel, that they should bring forth him that had cursed out of the camp, and stone him with stones. And the children of Israel did as the Lord commanded Moses.

According to an old Midrashic tradition, the 'Egyptian man' of Exodus and that of Leviticus are one and the same person. Or, to put it more clearly: the wicked Egyptian killed by Moses on the eve of the Exodus is none other than the Egyptian father of the blasphemer stoned in the Leviticus narrative. Here is how the story supposedly unfolded:[17]

Act I: In Egypt during the slavery

Shelomith, daughter of Dibri, of the tribe of Dan, was an Israelite of very beautiful appearance and the wife of a Hebrew taskmaster. Every morning, the Egyptian overseers went to the dwelling of the ten taskmasters for whom they had responsibility to send them to work before the crowing of the cock. One day, the overseer in charge of Shelomith's husband fixed his gaze on her and found her very much to his taste. As usual, he packed the Hebrew taskmaster off to work. He himself returned immediately, took advantage of the confusion of the dark hour and lay with Shelomith, who took him (it is thought) for her husband.

Just as the Egyptian overseer is departing the scene of his crime, the husband returns home and surprises him. The husband asks his wife: 'Did he touch you?' She replies: 'Yes, but I thought it was you!' Finding himself caught out, the Egyptian overseer sends his slave back to work and begins to beat him with the intention of killing him. This is the scene of which Moses, having returned 'unto his brethren', is the scandalized witness (Exod 2:11).

As everyone knows, Moses is a prophet, and he has been a prophet since before God formally revealed himself to him in the burning bush. He is therefore quite capable of seeing something he has not directly witnessed. 'And he looked this way and that way' (Exod 2:12): by prophecy he sees what the 'Egyptian man' has done to the Hebrew slave 'here' – in his dwelling, under his own roof, with his wife – and what he is now doing to him 'there' – at work, tyrannizing him and striking him with intent to kill. Still by prophecy, Moses 'sees that there is no man' (Exod 2:12). His concern is not to ensure that there is 'no man' around, no potential witness of the act he is about to perform. No, what he 'sees' is that 'no man', no posterity of righteous people or proselytes, is ever to be expected from this man or his offspring down to the last generation.

After having duly consulted the angels, a kind of celestial court, Moses executes the sentence he had in mind, 'slays the Egyptian, and hides him in the sand' (Exod 2:12). Alas, Shelomith finds herself pregnant thanks to the evil one. And nine months later, she gives birth to a boy: the one we encounter as an adult and rebel in Leviticus, the correctly termed 'son of an Israelitish woman, whose father was an Egyptian man' (Lev 24:10). Curtain.

Act II: In the desert, many years later

'The son of an Israelitish woman, whose father was an Egyptian man', 'goes out' (Lev 24:10). From where? From Moses's court. A dispute has pitted him against 'a man of Israel' who is a member of the tribe of Dan.

The son of Shelomith and the Egyptian overseer had come to pitch his tent in the camp of the tribe of Dan, on the basis that his mother hailed from it. This right had been denied him by the Danites on the grounds that his maternal ancestry did not in fact give him any rights, the Law specifying that everyone should pitch camp 'by his own standard, with the ensign of their father's house' (Num 2:2). Our man is out of luck: he does not have a paternal house in Israel, because his father was Egyptian. Moses's court therefore quite logically rejects his request.

He 'goes out' highly aggrieved and 'blasphemes the name of the Lord, and curses' (Lev 24:11). Brought back before Moses and his court, the blasphemer is placed under guard while Moses consults the Lord about how to deal with such an offence. The penalty as indicated by God is a severe one: 'Bring forth him that hath cursed without the camp; and let all that heard him lay their hands upon his head, and let all the congregation stone him' (Lev 24:13). And so they do and so ends the son of Shelomith, daughter of Dibri of the tribe Dan, and of the 'Egyptian man'. A bleak end that only serves to confirm the correctness of Moses's old prophecy, according to which no posterity of righteous people or proselytes was to be expected from the man whom he had justly killed. Curtain.

This fine, grim story is disturbing in several respects. In it the fate of 'the son . . . whose father was an Egyptian' (and whose mother, Shelomith, was an Israelite) seems to be closely associated with that of Moses. The latter is present at each crucial stage of this perverse family trajectory. He executes the father, the 'Egyptian man' who is the rapist of an Israelite and the would-be murderer of a Hebrew slave. And then he has that man's son stoned for blasphemy, many years later. But we still need to go beyond the simple narrative game thus set in motion, the strangely mechanical, almost determinist intertwining of plots. The invariably dramatic juxtaposition of Moses, the 'Egyptian man' and his son is obviously not merely intended to surprise or captivate readers. It highlights, as if the point needed making, the disquieting homology between the fates of Moses and of the blasphemer. In it, the blasphemer appears as the inverted figure or negative double of Moses himself.

This assertion obviously has considerable implications. But these are even greater than we might imagine. In fact, what the Midrash says of the history and family antecedents of the blasphemer in Leviticus is said, almost word for word, of Jesus himself by medieval Jewish counter-gospels – those polemical, singularly violent, Jewish parodies of Christian gospel stories. Here, summarized, is the story of the impure conception of the founder of Christianity as told by medieval Jews to themselves:

> Miriam (Mary), who lived with her mother, a poor widow, was a young woman of remarkable beauty, engaged to a certain Yohanan, a young man who was 'modest, humble and God-fearing'. Alas, she lived around the corner from a sinister character, Joseph Pandera, who spent his life 'in adultery, intrigue, theft and violence'. Joseph became besotted with the beautiful Miriam. One night, under cover of darkness, he broke into her house and she confused him with her fiancé. He slept with her twice, even though it was her period of menstrual impurity. Three months later, Yohanan clearly saw that his fiancée was pregnant, divined who was responsible, and fled to Babylon. The child was born and very early on displayed unbounded insolence towards the Sages of his time. His identity was revealed and he was declared a *mamzer* (bastard), the son of a *niddah* (impure woman). He was dubbed Yeshu, an abbreviation of the phrase 'May his name and memory be erased!'[18] Thus began the career of Jesus, who claimed to be 'born of a virgin' and the 'son of God', a great blasphemer in the sight of the Everlasting God and destined for an infamous death: stoning (followed by hanging).

Having clarified this, readers will be aware that whatever I now say of Moses and the blasphemer in Leviticus also applies in effect to Moses and Jesus (at least as recast by medieval Judaism). The blasphemer in Leviticus as the negative double of Moses; Jesus as the negative double of Moses. All this goes together.

In Leviticus, the blasphemer has no name. He is simply the 'son of'. As we have seen, 'Jesus' is not a name either, but the opposite of one – the erasure of any name. As for Moses, readers will recall that he remained unnamed for a long time, becoming 'Moses' only belatedly, on the initiative of one or other of his mothers. The blasphemer and Jesus are both children abandoned by their fathers. Moses, too, is an abandoned infant, but he is not altogether deserted and he even gets adopted. Familial deficit on the one hand, over-compensation on the other. The blasphemer and Jesus are born of an adulterous union and indeed of rape (possibly consensual sex, but this is not very clear). Moses is born to two members of the tribe of Levi bound in a perfectly legitimate union. He nevertheless finds himself adopted by the daughter of his people's emblematic enemy (Pharaoh). The blasphemer's identity is dual, but split, and it excludes him: the son of an Israelite and an Egyptian, he finds no place in the camp; the community rejects him and finally stones him to death. The identity of Jesus as an illegitimate child, a *mamzer*, although effectively an 'Israelite' (Jewish), prevents him 'enter[ing] into the congregation of the Lord even to [the] tenth generation' (according to Deut 23:3). The community, at first divided by his preaching, rejects him, just as it will later expel all his followers from its ranks; it ends up stoning him. Moses's identity is likewise, if not split, then certainly dual and possible triple (Hebrew, Egyptian, husband of a Midianite). And yet – for here the parallel becomes an absolute contrast – Moses does not turn into a blasphemer or the founder of a heretical Church, but quite the opposite: a prophet of the Everlasting One and the greatest of them all. He becomes the head of his community. And it is he who orders the sowers of disorder and division in its ranks to be stoned.

The genealogical fragility and ambiguity of Moses – what is Moses the name of? Whom is Moses the son of? – become a source of strength in him. What marked him out, and might have excluded him from the community, ensures his integration into it; and what roots him in the community in no way prevents his anchorage in the Universal, but on the contrary guarantees it. How is this possible?

'The Man Moses'

Moses, Jew; Moses, non-Jew: he is henceforth wholly the one and wholly the other – able to be wholly the one only by being wholly the other. Jewish – doubly, triply Jewish: the son of two members of the tribe of Levi, the adoptive son of Bithiah the convert, and through her the adoptive grandson of the God whose prophet he is. Non-Jewish – doubly, triply non-Jewish: the adoptive son of an Egyptian woman, the husband of Zipporah the Midianite, the son-in-law of Jethro the idolatrous priest, and adoptive grandson of Pharaoh himself, the enemy of his people, whose destruction he consummates. Whereas, in the figure of the blasphemer as in that of Jesus, there is uncertainty about identity in the form of subtraction and division, in the case of Moses it is sublimated in addition and realized in unity – of the Jewish people, but also of humanity.

Moses is definitely not a 'Jewish Jew'. Nor, happily, is he an 'authentic Jew'. He is an Egyptian Jew – all the more Jewish because he is Egyptian, and all the more of a human being because he is both. Moses is the Hebrew who goes among 'his brethren', sees their suffering and endeavours to remedy it. But Moses is also the 'Egyptian man' (*ish mitzri*) who rescues the daughters of the Midianite priest from violent shepherds. And being both the one and the other, he is also, paradigmatically, principally, a man. He is 'the man Moses', *ha-ish Mosheh*. Moses is in fact referred to thus four times in the Pentateuch.

The first time it is as the leader of the Hebrews and in the eyes of the Egyptians. We are in Egypt on the eve of the tenth and last plague: the death of the first-born. The country has already endured nine terrible scourges. Despite this, God 'gave the [Hebrew] people favour in the sight of the Egyptians' (Exod 11:3). The same verse adds: 'Moreover, the man Moses [*ha-ish Mosheh*] was very great in the land of Egypt, in the sight of Pharaoh's servants, and in the sight of the people.'

The second time it is as the son-in-law of Jethro, the Midianite. Israel has escaped from Egypt. Jethro joins Moses in the desert, near the mountain of the Lord, accompanied by Zipporah and the two children she has borne the prophet: 'And Moses went out to meet his father in law, and did obeisance, and kissed him; and they asked each other of their welfare' (Exod 18:7). Or, literally, 'each man [*ish*] asked his fellow [*re'ehu*] about his health'. Rashi tells us that *ish* here is Moses. Here is the prophet's simplicity, his modesty even, as a man among men, taking the Midianite simply for his fellow man (and if Jethro will one day convert, as Tradition would have it, he has not done so yet).

The third time it is as the one who has liberated Israel from slavery and in the sight of Israel itself. Moses is on the Lord's mountain, where he receives the Law and where God gives him the two Tablets of Testimony, stone tables engraved by his finger. Moses lingers and the people become worried, anxious, and ask Aaron to fashion replacement gods (the Golden Calf). Israel is about to betray Moses and nonetheless expresses itself thus: 'this Moses, the man [*ha-ish*] that brought us out of the land of Egypt, we wot not what is become of him' (Exod 32:1).

Fourthly, and finally, in the sight of the Everlasting God himself and as his servant. Miriam and Aaron have just maligned Moses. They rebel, or at least question themselves: 'Hath the Lord indeed spoken only by Moses? Hath he not also spoken by us?' (Num 12:2). Is Moses not overdoing things? Is he not presumptuous? God's anger is on the point of exploding against them. He is ready to remind them that, of all his house, Moses is unquestionably the most faithful; that he speaks to him 'mouth to mouth', clearly, without mysteries; and that Moses, and Moses alone, contemplates his image. But the first thing recalled by the text on the subject of the prophet is this: 'Now the man Moses was very meek, above all the men which were upon the face of the earth' (Num 12:3). Moses: a man among men, and the meekest of them all.

In the man Moses, greatness and humility are one. All human beings, whether they are Israelites, Midianites or Egyptians; whether he punishes them or liberates them; whether he is their brother, son-in-law, husband, leader or adversary; and even when they are on the verge of treachery and rebellion, all of them recognize – or are compelled to recognize – the fusion in him of grandeur and humility. All recognize, or are compelled to recognize, in Moses what makes him perfectly human. Prophet of the Everlasting God, first among Hebrews, son of the Egyptian woman – although he is all that, and because he is all that, Moses always remains 'the man Moses'. Perfect as a man; imperfect because he is a man. His frailty is his strength. But his strength never overrides his frailty. For Moses, because he is a man, may die at any moment, leaving his mission unfulfilled.

3

Journey, Night, Death

Three verses of terror and darkness. Three, no more. They seem to interrupt the narrative, create a strange disorder in it and, worse, suddenly open up a gaping hole, possibly an abyss.

God has addressed Moses from the burning bush and, after trying to get out of it, Moses has finally accepted the mission God entrusts him with. He will leave the desert of Midian, give up the peaceful life he has lived as an obscure shepherd with Jethro, his father-in-law, and Zipporah his wife. He must return to Egypt, where he is not short of enemies; find his brother Aaron, who will be his companion and spokesman; and present himself before Pharaoh. He is aware that the road will be long and hard, even if he knows that the outcome of the coming battle is a certainty. He sees his father-in-law one last time, takes leave of him, and sets off: 'And Moses took his wife and his sons, and set them upon an ass, and he returned into the land of Egypt' (Exod 4:20). In his hand, he holds the staff of miracles.

Then suddenly, at once, without transition, these famous three verses of terror and darkness (Exod 4:24–26). Three, no more.

Here is a first translation, that of the King James Bible:

> And it came to pass by the way in the inn, that the Lord met him, and sought to kill him (Exod 4:24). Then Zipporah took a sharp stone, and cut off the foreskin of her son, and cast it at his feet, and said, Surely a bloody husband art thou to me. (25). So he let him go: then she said, A bloody husband thou art, because of the circumcision. (26)

And here is a second translation, that of Robert Alter (2004):[1]

> And it happened on the way at the night camp that the Lord encountered him and sought to put him to death (24). And Zipporah took a flint and cut off her son's foreskin and touched it to his feet, and she said: 'Yes, a bridegroom of blood you are to me' (25). And He let him go. Then did she say: 'A bridegroom of blood by the circumcising' (26).

And here is a third, that of André Chouraqui (1974):

> And it is on the road, at the inn: IHVH meets him and seeks to do him to death (24). Zipporah takes a flint, cut off the foreskin of her son, and with it touches him at his feet. She says: 'Yes, you are to me a husband of blood' (25). He lets him go. Then she says: 'A husband of blood, by the circumcisions!' (26).[2]

I could cite other translations – Jewish, Christian, respectful or otherwise of the results of modern historico-critical science, concerned or not with literary elegance, seeking to reproduce the bizarre flavour of the Hebraic original or not. This would not change much. The upshot would hardly be different: the further the narrative progresses, the more it equivocates.

So let start at the beginning and not be afraid of feeling our way forwards, through an ever darker night.

Exodus Chapter 4, Verses 24–26

The first of the three verses is the clearest. This is how I would render it: 'As he was on his way, at the night stage, God approached him, wanting to do him to death.' Same clarity for the start of the second: 'Zipporah took hold of a stone, cut off the outgrowth [= the foreskin] of her son.' Thereafter things become complicated. The sequel, one and a half verses, slips through our fingers.

The immediate continuation, first of all: 'she touched/caused to touch/deposited at his feet' (Exod 4:25). The subject of the verb is, in all likelihood, Zipporah, who has just circumcised her son. The action described, on the other hand, is unclear. The verb, which is transitive, probably means more than simply 'touch', but something like 'makes touch', 'brings into contact'. But it has no explicit object. So, what does Zipporah put in contact and with what? Difficult to say. Obviously, it is very tempting to gloss over the gaps and construe it as follows: '[Zipporah] made [her son's foreskin] touch his feet.' But this is a little hasty and ultimately resolves nothing. In Hebrew, the possessive adjective is masculine; it therefore cannot be Zipporah's feet. But whose then? God's? Moses's? The infant's? To further confuse matters, the phrase I have translated by 'at his feet' could also mean 'before him'. Doing some violence to the meaning of the verb, and adding to it an object that is not specified, would make it possible to read: '[Zipporah] deposited [her son's foreskin] at his feet.' That said, we are scarcely any further forward: we still do not know whose 'feet' are being referred to.

The end of the second verse (Exod 24:5) is even more disquieting. Zipporah is not content to act, but also speaks: 'She says: "In fact, you are to me a *hatan* of bloods."' We do not know to whom she is talking (only that it is to a male being): Moses, her son, God? I put 'bloods' in the plural to render an enigmatic plural in Hebrew (*damim*). Finally, I have not translated the word *hatan* because its meaning here is doubtful. In the Book of Exodus, it only appears twice, precisely in the present context. We find it elsewhere in Scripture where it is usually rendered by 'son-in-law', 'fiancé', 'husband' or 'ally'. At first sight, it is difficult to pin down exactly what it means here.

Finally, we have the third and last verse (Exod 4:26). 'He released him. Then she said: "a *hatan* of bloods, for the circumcision."' It is probably God who 'releases' Moses. What I perhaps translate rather freely by 'circumcision' is the Hebrew *mulot*. This word, which appears to be a noun, does not feature in this form anywhere else in the Bible, but seems based on a root that we find in the Hebrew verbs for 'to circumcise' or 'to be circumcised'. As for the phrase '*hatan* of bloods', which returns for a second time in Zipporah's mouth, it is as obscure here as in the preceding verse; I shall therefore say nothing about it.

That's it, then. We have not understood a thing, or almost nothing, and who can blame us? We will be told nothing more. Immediately afterwards, the narrative resumes its normal course and recovers its habitual fluidity and lucidity. God tells Moses to go and meet his brother Aaron in the desert. He goes, finds him and embraces him. The two of them present themselves before the Elders of Israel, relay the Lord's words to the people, and perform various miracles in public. The people believe them.

They present themselves for the first time before Pharaoh (Exod 4:27–5:1). And so forth.

To characterize these three strange verses, which I have had such difficulty translating (but we have seen that I am not alone in this), I have spoken of a gaping hole. Because what they relate (but what *do* they relate?) seems to lack any clear, direct link with either what precedes them or what ensues. As if they were a parenthesis, which could just as well be skipped. Yet we have to recognize that the ultimate compiler of the text of the Bible did not skip this passage. He left it in, profoundly awkward for sure, but he left it in. And it is up to us to resolve things.

I also referred to three verses of darkness. I mean this in three senses. It happens 'at night'. The Hebrew is obscure. It speaks to us of death. Suddenly, in the very middle of the night, Moses (if it is indeed him) is going (obscurely) to die. It is God who wants to do him to death. And if God fulfils his murderous desire, the narrative – the whole narrative – will stop there. For good. It is therefore impossible to ignore these three verses of terror and darkness. Because the whole narrative, all the rest of the narrative, hangs on them. Rather than a black hole, these verses are perhaps the key to it.

And, whatever I might have said, things are not completely obscure. Let us therefore forget what we do not know for the time being. And let us rely on what we do know with something approximating certainty; on what gleams forth in this darkness despite everything.

The place and time, first of all. We are travelling ('on the way') between two sites – Midian and Egypt – in the no-man's-land that is the desert or mountain; and it is night. We are at a staging post (*ba-malon*), somewhere travellers stop to spend the night – in a 'caravansary', the Targum* will say.

Next, the characters. Main character: God, or maybe just [an angel of] God, Abraham Ibn Ezra* observing that it is not uncommon for Scripture to call God someone who is in fact merely his messenger. Second character: Moses, most probably, though he is not formally named. It is probably him whom God wishes to put to death (as we shall see, however, this is not the view of all commentators). Third character: a son of Moses, whose name is not indicated here. Is it the older one, Gershom, whose birth was mentioned in Chapter 2 of Exodus? Or is it the younger, Eliezer, of whom no mention has been made as yet, and who will only be introduced much later (Exod 18:4)? Probably the younger, who has just been born and must therefore be circumcised without delay. Fourth and final character: Zipporah, Moses's Midianite wife, who has borne him two children, and who is the only one of the four to speak.

Now, the action and the dialogue. A character (presumably Moses) is threatened with death by God (or his messenger). And it is by circumcising their son that Zipporah saves her husband from death. She speaks twice: the first time after performing the circumcision, the second time after God (or his messenger) has 'released' Moses. On both occasions, she clearly seems to address someone: 'You are to me . . .', without it being easy to determine who (God, Moses, her son?). Both times she uses the phrase '*hatan* of bloods'. But this phrase, whose reference is not obvious, appearing at two different points in the action and in two sentences that are differently formulated, perhaps has a different meaning each time – one that would be difficult to determine a priori, anyway.

The crux and stake of the plot, finally, are plain enough. It is a matter of life and death: the life and death of Moses, or possibly his son. Nothing is said at first about the cause, the reasons for the threat that hangs over the prophet or his son: [the angel of] God says nothing, he threatens. On the other hand, we know what it is that saves whoever is threatened with death: the circumcision of Zipporah's son.

The circumcision injunction has hitherto only been mentioned once, in the Book of Genesis, when God prescribes it to Abraham as a 'token of the covenant' between God and his posterity, the uncircumcised Hebrew henceforth at risk of being 'cut off' because (says the Lord) 'he hath broken my covenant' (Gen 17:14). Only here, at this curious moment in the cycle of the accounts of Moses's life, does it appear again. It is what ultimately permits us to exclude the possibility that the person mortally threatened in Exodus 4:24 is Moses's son.

This reading exists, of course. According to Abraham Ibn Ezra, Samuel ben Hofni (d. 1013) puts it thus: 'Far be it from us to entertain the idea that God wanted to kill Moses, the very man who is on his way to accomplish the mission [entrusted to him by God] of delivering his people! He only wanted to kill Eliezer [his son].' However, it is not hard to rule out such an interpretation. There seems no reason for such an abrupt character switch: the person on his 'way' is Moses, clearly the referent in the preceding passage; his wife and children are merely accompanying him. Why, all of a sudden, should someone else – the son of the main character – be the referent, without it being specified (explicit mention is made of this son only subsequently, when his mother circumcises him). Next, if Moses retains freedom of movement (if he has not been assaulted by the divine messenger), how do we explain him delegating to a woman – his wife Zipporah – the circumcision of his son? Furthermore, if Eliezer had suddenly found himself in mortal danger, would it have been reasonable to subject him to a surgical act that could only weaken him further?

Similarly, what sense would there be in abruptly making Eliezer the central hero of a narrative, when this character (like Gershom for that matter) will not subsequently play any role in the story of Israel or even in the life of Moses? Finally, and above all, is it not, exegetically speaking, far more interesting to think that it is none other than Moses whom God wanted to do to death?

Incomprehensible, shocking, at the very least absurd? None of this should give us pause. On the contrary. Yes, God wished for the death of the one whom he had just made his prophet, and whom he had charged with leading his people out of Egypt. And yes, Moses, future artisan of the Covenant that would be sealed between God and his people on Sinai, had earlier violated the covenant of circumcision, sealed between God and the ancestor of this people, Abraham. The challenge is overwhelming, agreed, but it is precisely this kind of challenge that an interpreter worthy of the name aspires to meet.

Under the Sway of the Law

For some, this sombre narrative is there only to remind us of the capital importance of the circumcision commandment. Of such importance that even the immense merits of the first and greatest of the prophets counted for nothing when it turned out he had neglected its observance, or even that he had merely deferred its execution. Because he is ultimately accused not so much of negligence as of having been slow to act.

In his defence, it seems that Moses found himself torn between two imperatives and two divine commandments. The one, specifically addressing him, concerns his departure: 'Go, return into Egypt' (Exod 4:19). The other, incumbent on every Hebrew father, is to circumcise a male child eight days after birth. For Eliezer, his second son, had only just been born.

There is indeed a tradition, as already mentioned,[3] according to which Moses supposedly made an agreement with Jethro, his father-in-law, reserving his first-born for idol worship and the next for worship of the One True God. In this case, the incident might well involve Gershom, who is no longer breastfeeding, and who has deliberately been sacrificed by his father to idolatry. Perhaps reluctantly, if we are to believe the words that the Targum* puts in the mouth of Zipporah, addressing the Exterminating Angel:[4] '*My* husband (*hatan*) *wanted to circumcise him, but his father-in-law would not let him. And now* the blood (*damim*) of this circumcision *has expiated the sins of this husband here!*'[5] Liberated from any commitment to Jethro by his departure, and now free to act, at worst Moses was late circumcising Gershom.

This second option is not unappealing. It would make it possible to dramatize, just as he is returning to Egypt, Moses's final and definitive rupture – under divine pressure and in the context of a radical test – with what, in and around him, is not Jewish. The two sons whom he has had with the Midianite are now circumcised. In addition, it is the Midianite herself who has circumcised the older one. This being done, Moses remains alive. Or rather, he changes his life. At last he is the unsullied Hebrew he should be. And, on this basis, he can begin to carry out the mission assigned him by God.

Apparently so convenient, this scenario is nonetheless somewhat disturbing. Abraham Ibn Ezra, for one, rejects it categorically. How can we, for one second, believe that Moses could have made such an agreement with Zipporah and his father-in-law, involving such a compromise with idolatry? 'A prophet would not act thus. Still less the greatest of the prophets.' His offence must be less grave. In the case of the greatest of prophets, this would not prevent it from incurring the death penalty (as it would in the case of the average believer, of whom less rigour is required). A fault, then, but if possible slight. If we search hard enough, we shall find it.

Moses must set off. Eliezer has just been born. Will the prophet circumcise the infant and depart straight away, accomplishing simultaneously, without delay, the two divine commands – the general and the particular – incumbent on him? To set off immediately, with an infant who has just been circumcised, would not be advisable. A circumcised child is unwell for three days at least. Yet to circumcise an infant and wait three days for it to recover is not possible either, without deferring execution of the divine commandment to leave for Egypt.

Moses therefore decides to set off at once, accompanied by his wife and children, reckoning that he cannot postpone his departure without contravening God's explicit order. But, relying on an old and duly attested tradition according to which an infant cannot – indeed must not – be circumcised at eight days if he is to accompany on their travels those responsible for him, and who cannot put off their journey, Moses postpones the circumcision of his son. In so doing, he believes he is acting in accordance with the Law.

Let us grant that such is indeed the case. If he has committed an offence, he must have done so after departing. This is what is suggested by Rashi.[6] Once he is on his way, and has thus begun to carry out the divine command to depart at once, finding himself already somewhat in compliance on this score, perhaps he should have taken advantage of the first staging post to circumcise the son born to him straight away (even if it meant stopping there three days for the infant to recover). His only fault would then be that on reaching the inn he concerned himself with his lodging (*malon*) before circumcising his son.

However, Abraham Ibn Ezra does not support this view. According to him, the prophet's offence lies elsewhere. He situates it earlier on, at the very moment Moses set off. Had he paid more attention to the divine order to leave, he would have left on his own. At no point does God ask him to go with his wife and children. He said but one thing to him: 'Go, return into Egypt' (Exod 4:19), in the singular. By taking his family with him, Moses has put himself in a difficult position and under an obligation to manage, with the least possible harm, the tension he has created between two equally imperative obligations, whose performance will brook no delay (departure and circumcision). That is why God sends his Angel: so that Moses will abandon this calculation, proceed forthwith to the circumcision of his son, and set out at once himself, leaving his wife and convalescent son behind. The threat of death hanging over him takes the form of a sudden malady. Understanding that his survival depends on the circumcision of his son, but with his illness causing his hand to tremble, it is to his wife Zipporah that he entrusts the performance of the act. Moses is cured. And now, from here, he departs alone for Egypt.

We know for certain that Zipporah and the two children never accompanied their husband and father to Egypt and never experienced the wounds of slavery and escape from it alongside him. It is for this very reason that much later, after the Exodus, we see Jethro, accompanied by Zipporah, Gershom and Eliezer, set forth from Midian to find Moses in the desert: 'Then Jethro, Moses' father in law, took Zipporah, Moses's wife, *after he had sent her back*, and her two sons . . . unto Moses into the wilderness, where he encamped at the mount of God' (Exod 18:2-5). It is manifestly after the episode we are concerned with – our three enigmatic verses – that Moses sent back (to the country of Midian) his wife and two sons, returning to Egypt alone.

All this is, in fact, already clearly stated by the very verse that describes Moses's return into Egypt in a single sentence: 'And Moses took his wife and his sons, and set them upon an ass, and he returned to the land of Egypt' (Exod 4:20). This should be understood as follows: 'Moses [*first*] took his wife and sons, and set them upon an ass [*but then, after the circumcision of the younger one, on his own*] returned to the land of Egypt.' It is written: 'he returned', in the singular; not: 'they returned'.

This interpretation has its advantages. Not the least of them is that it restores Moses, relieved of his family after a brief moment of distraction, to the absolute solitude of the unique prophet selected by God for a unique mission. In the light of it, the narrative also seems to play the indirect role of completing, as it were, and albeit at the risk of his death, Moses's 'training' as both jurist and prophet. The first commandment communicated by God to Moses was: 'Go, return into Egypt' (Exod 4:19). He has just learned that not a single detail in divine discourse is superfluous. He should have appreciated that the commandment was formulated in the singular, not the plural. And, had he been more attentive, he would never have put himself in the position of neglecting (or seeming to neglect) the circumcision commandment. Moses will learn this lesson. He will not forget it – save on one occasion, many years later, as we shall see, and then, yes, he will die.[7]

Although this interpretation has its advantages, it imprisons us in a strictly legalistic interpretation of the passage that concerns us. At stake in it is little more than the Law: understanding the Law and obeying it. Circumcision is a commandment and, ultimately, is only valuable as such. For the ancient rabbis, it was a fundamental commandment: any major anti-Jewish persecution was accompanied by – even essentially translated into – a ban on circumcision. Consequently, it was an act of spiritual and communal resistance, an exemplary act reasserting the primacy of the Law that grounded the group's existence and ensured its cohesion. (In this regard, by – happily – renouncing circumcision, Christians sealed their definitive rupture with Judaism.) Moses's offence is not to have obeyed this commandment. A fault that is punishable by death – at least for him. As soon as the commandment is obeyed (in the event, by someone other than Moses: his wife), everything returns to normal: the sanction is lifted and Moses is safe.

However, whatever people may say, there is something incomplete about this. Is it the observance – by Zipporah at the last moment – of a commandment (here, circumcision) neglected by Moses that saves him from the death penalty hanging over him? Or – and this is entirely different – is it the specific, distinctive act of circumcision (and that alone), the blood shed by the circumcised infant, that saves Moses from death? This second possibility obliges us to go beyond the familiar territory of the legality of the Law, and enter the more mysterious territory of the effectivity of its practice. Is to worship a God simply to obey him and escape malediction? Or is it much more than that: to shatter the divine verdict, force God's hand, and wrest his blessing from him?

The Blood of the Sacrifice

The advent of Christianity, its recuperation of the symbolism of the Paschal Lamb, its valorization of Christ's self-sacrifice, its assertion of the redemptive efficacy of the blood shed by the

Son – none of this ever prompted Judaism to react by simply denying the sacrificial value of the blood of circumcision and exclusively privileging a definition of circumcision as communal rite and fundamental commandment of the Law. The destruction of the Second Temple and the disappearance of its worship in 70 CE left circumcision as perhaps the sole sacrificial rite of Judaism, or one of the few. Blood has flowed, does flow, and will flow. And it will never flow in vain. Zipporah herself reminds us of this. Twice, and both times in the plural, she utters the word 'blood(s)' (*damim*).

Let us once again, then, take up the thread of the story. Zipporah, mother of the infant and wife of Moses, seizes a 'stone' (*tsor*) – a sharp stone.

The word *tsor* in fact evokes a phrase in the Book of Joshua, which appears in a context not unrelated to ours. Israel has just crossed the River Jordan and God asks Joshua, Moses's successor, to proceed to the circumcision of all his people's males. Joshua takes 'sharp knives' (*harvot tsurim*) and 'circumcises the children of Israel at the hill of the *Aralot*' – the 'hill of the foreskins' (Josh 5:3). The males circumcised by Joshua are the men of Israel born in the desert. Their fathers, who were circumcised, have all perished during the forty years of their peregrinations between Egypt and Canaan. The new generation has not been able to perform this duty during the trek, 'on the way', *ba-derekh* (Josh 5:5).[8] They now proceed with the rite and remain in the camp until they have recovered. This allows God to exclaim: 'This day have I rolled away the reproach of Egypt from off you' (Josh 5:9). Israel is now ready to take possession of the Land promised to it and celebrates its first Passover there.

Zipporah thus does to her son precisely what Joshua will much later do to Israel: she takes a 'sharp stone', circumcises the infant, cuts off his 'outgrowth' (*orlah*), removes the last vestige of Gentility from him, and purifies him of 'the reproach of Egypt'. Although this is not exactly clarified, she deposits this outgrowth 'at his feet' or causes it to touch them. Whose? The infant's? Moses's? Those of the Angel of the Lord who seeks to kill the latter?

Zipporah has evidently understood which offence Moses risks paying for with his life: non-circumcision of his son. And that is why she exclaims: 'Surely a husband of bloods [*hatan damim*] art thou to me' (Exod 4:25). According to commentators, she is addressing her son and referring to him: 'In effect, she means by this: you are the reason why the blood of my husband could be shed!' Observing that she is not mistaken, and that performance of the commandment of circumcision persuades the Angel of Death to release Moses, she once again exclaims: 'A husband of bloods thou art, because of the circumcision' (Exod 4:26). Which means: 'Yes, the blood of my husband was nearly shed because of the circumcision!' Or, unless Zipporah has not simply repeated herself: 'My husband is still alive thanks to the blood of this circumcision!'

These two interpretations of Zipporah's second exclamation are far from equivalent. The first suggests that non-execution of a commandment earned Moses a possible death sentence, while its execution led to him escaping that penalty. It simply operates on the legal level: violation of the Law is punishable by a sanction that observance of the Law lifts. The second interpretation has a quite different import. It suggests that what prevents Moses's blood being shed is the bloodshed of the circumcision. As Abraham Ibn Ezra notes, 'bloods' (*damim*) can be construed in two senses: the murder, death, spilled blood (real or metaphorical) of someone – such as Moses – whom one wishes to put to death; or, blood in the strict, primary sense – such as the blood shed by the circumcision of his son. The son's 'bloodshed' (circumcision) enables the father's blood not to be shed (enables Moses not to die). It is not mere observance of the Law that spares Moses his penalty. It is the sacrifice of the son's blood that spares the father from death.

These two readings are obviously not mutually exclusive. Just as Judaism does not choose between conceiving worship as observance of the Law and conceiving it as theurgical practice, nor does it choose between circumcision as commandment and circumcision as sacrifice. On the other hand, depending on the context, milieu or author, the stress can shift and the balance between the two vary.

While some rabbinical teachings stress the pre-eminence of circumcision as a legal disposition ('great is circumcision, which weighs as much as all the commandments of the Torah'[9]), others attest to the salvific, protective value traditionally attached to it. Some legendary accounts thus evoke Abraham, the first circumcised man, posted at the entrance to Gehenna ensuring that no circumcised male of Israel enters there – except for sinners, of course, onto whom he grafts the foreskins collected from Jewish infants who died before they were eight days old (hence before they could be circumcised), and who as a result, in a happy combination, escape Hell. In the Middle Ages, we find Rashbam* endeavouring to hold both ends of the string together. Believing that it was 'at the feet of' Moses (who is saved) that the bloody foreskin of his son (who saves him) was laid, or that it was placed in contact with them, this exegete clearly highlights the sacrificial dimension of Zipporah's act, while recalling its legal dimension: '[Performance of] this *commandment* [circumcision] enabled Moses to be saved, as [would] a *sacrifice*.'

Ibn Ezra is much more precise: he establishes an explicit link between the episode of the circumcision of Moses's son and the first Passover. Zipporah stains 'the feet' of Moses with the blood of the circumcision of his son, just as the Hebrews will later stain the lintels and posts of their doors with the blood of the Paschal Lamb. In Moses's case, as in that of his people, the sight of the blood from the sacrifice (circumcision or lamb) stays God's hand. In one instance, he renounces killing a Moses stained with the blood of his son's circumcision. In the other, when 'at midnight' (Exod 12:29) he causes all the first-born in the land of Egypt to perish, he passes over the houses of the Hebrews marked with the blood of the lamb and thereby spares their children. The blood of the sacrificed lamb is a 'ransom' or 'expiation' (*kofer*), protecting those who sacrificed it. The blood from the circumcision of Moses's son works the exact same way for Moses.

The parallel doubtless asserts itself. It is worth noting that the account of Moses's ordeal (Exod 4:24–6) is immediately preceded by God's announcement, addressing the prophet just before his departure from Midian, of the final plague – the tenth – that will strike Egypt: 'And the Lord said unto Moses, When thou goest to return into Egypt, see that thou do all those wonders before Pharaoh, which I have put in thine hand: but I will harden his heart, that he shall not let the people go. And thou shalt say unto Pharaoh, Thus saith the Lord, Israel is my son, even my firstborn: And I say unto thee, Let my son go, that he may serve me: and if thou refuse to let him go, behold, I will slay thy son, even thy firstborn' (Exod 4:21-3). The firstborn of Egypt shall perish. The firstborns of Israel – itself the firstborn of God – will escape death by virtue of the spilled blood of the lamb.

Viewed in this light, our three verses of darkness take on a meaning of unexpected clarity. And from the terror they initially

inspired in us there ultimately emerges an astonishingly redemptive prospect. Far from snapping the narrative thread, as might
be thought on a first reading, they tie the threads of a deeper
continuity. Abraham is the father of Israel. Moses is its teacher.
The former grounds Jewish identity in genealogy; the second in
adhesion to the Torah. Circumcision is the token of a first
Covenant, contracted vertically by God with Abraham and his
descendants in Canaan, before the birth of Isaac. The Torah
bears testimony to a second Covenant, the confirmation of the
first, contracted horizontally by God with the whole community
of Israel after the exodus from Egypt, in the desert, and through
the intermediary of Moses. Our three verses of darkness and
terror tie all this up together. Moses inscribes himself in the
continuity of the Abrahamic covenant: he (re)lives in his flesh
and his son's the ordeal of circumcision, as a ritual act at once
foundational and redemptive. At the same time, he is already
inscribed in the time of the future covenant: he undergoes,
individually and in advance, a fundamentally paschal experience, a prefiguration of what will later be collectively lived by all
the children of Israel, henceforth under his guidance. It may be
that these three verses of darkness and terror celebrate nothing
other than the union in them of Abraham and Moses, of Moses
and his people, of the blood that saves and the Law that preserves
from death – a blood and a Law that we shall encounter once
again during the final, (re)founding consecration of Sinai:

> And Moses came [from the mountain] and told the people
> all the words of the Lord, and all the judgments: and all the
> people answered with one voice, and said, All the words
> which the Lord hath said will we do. And Moses wrote all
> the words of the Lord, and rose up early in the morning,

and builded an altar under the hill, and twelve pillars, according to the twelve tribes of Israel. And he sent young men of the children of Israel, which offered burnt offerings, and sacrificed peace offerings of oxen unto the Lord. And Moses took half of the blood, and put it in basins; and half of the blood he sprinkled on the altar. And he took the book of the covenant*, and read in the audience of the people: and they said, All that the Lord hath said we will do, and be obedient. And Moses took the blood, and sprinkled it on the people, and said, Behold the blood of the covenant, which the Lord hath made with you concerning all these words (Exod 24:3–8).

A Hostile God

From behind the express narrative frame – the story of Moses's life – another, more profound one thus emerges. While they seemed to abruptly interrupt the first frame, and create a terrifying black hole in it, our three verses suddenly ensure the continuity of the second and illuminate it. This conversion of darkness into light and arbitrariness into necessity is certainly appealing. But is it sufficient? Is it even wholly legitimate? Does it truly dispel the unease that grips readers when they come upon these famous three verses? For the unease is still there, persistent, stubbornly resistant to any exegetical strategy, however subtle or ingenious. A fact – the stuff of scandal – remains: just after choosing him as his prophet and assigning a mission to him, God 'seeks to kill' Moses.

Curiously, what shocks us about this no longer seems so shocking when it does not involve Moses. A structurally similar scenario, albeit different in its tonality, does not arouse the same sense of indignation when the victim is someone else. That

someone is Balaam, Moses's parodic double. The Book of
Numbers tells his story. Thanks to the contrast it affords, it may
serve to enlighten us as to the meaning of the ordeal inflicted on
Moses – or at least as to the nature of the disturbance it creates
in us.

After forty years of wandering in the desert, the Hebrews are
at the gates of Canaan. They have just defeated the Amorites and
the king of Bashan. It is now that Balaam comes on the scene.
He is a prophet – a prophet of the Gentiles, certainly, but nevertheless duly visited by the Lord who has granted him some
enlightenment. Such is his reputation indeed that Balak, king of
Moab, alarmed by the Hebrews' victorious advance, wants to
persuade him to come and curse the people of Israel. A curse
uttered by this prophet would, in his view, have every chance of
coming true. Balak sends emissaries. Balaam, apparently reluctant to get involved without taking precautions, consults the
Lord, who forbids him to follow the envoys of the Moabite king
and warns him: 'Thou shalt not curse the people [of Israel]: for
they are blessed' (Num 22:12). Balak and his emissaries insist.
God finally tells Balaam: 'Rise up, and go with them' (Num
22:20). But it is clear from that moment that Balaam will only
be able to do what God dictates to him. And so it proves, to the
chagrin of King Balak: the divine spirit will seize Balaam every
time he wishes to utter his oracles, and he will bless Israel rather
than cursing it.

Balaam is, to say the least, an ambiguous character. Despite
himself, he blesses those whom he is asked to curse. The biblical
and, subsequently, rabbinical tradition will go further. It will
accuse him, *inter alia*, of having suggested to Israel's enemies an
infallible strategy for tripping it up: inciting it to debauchery and
idolatry. And, sure enough, once Balaam and Balak have

returned home, the people indulge in lechery with the girls of Moab and Midian and, at their instigation, agree to bow down before their gods. The punishment that will strike the sinners of Israel will be terrible and Balaam himself will perish by the sword (Num 31:8).

A prophet of truth despite himself, and however impure his ultimate aims, Balaam is no less a prophet. He is like Moses: an inverted, parodic and grotesque Moses, who undergoes – precisely in this mode: inverted, parodic and grotesque – an experience which, in many respects, seems modelled on Moses's own in our three verses of darkness.

The episode occurs at the start of Balaam's 'mission'. God seems finally to have ceded to his pleas and those of Balak's emissaries. He comes to Balaam 'at night' and intimates to him what resembles an order, a commandment: 'If the men come to call thee, rise up, and go with them; but yet the word which I shall say unto thee, that thou shalt do' (Num 22:20).

What does Balaam do? He complies and, even if he continues to harbour evil designs, he does exactly what God asks of him: 'And Balaam rose up in the morning, and saddled his ass, and went with the princes of Moab' (Num 22:21). Then, suddenly, we have the first divine volte-face: 'And God's anger was kindled because he went: and the angel of the Lord stood in the way for an adversary [*satan*] against him' (Num 22:22). This angel, 'his sword drawn in his hand' (Num 22:23), threatens Balaam with death. However, the latter sees nothing; he is unaware of being in danger and wishes to continue on his way. The she-ass sees the angel and his sword. It swerves, seeks to flee across the fields, traps its master's foot against the wall bordering the path, and finally lies down under Balaam. Balaam strikes his mount three times, without succeeding in getting it to move. The Lord opens the mouth of the ass, which addresses its master. Finally, he opens the eyes of Balaam, who sees the Angel. The Angel says: 'Wherefore hast thou smitten thine ass these three times? behold, it is I who came out as an adversary (*satan*), because thy way is perverse before me: And the ass saw me, and turned from me these three times: unless she had turned from me, surely now also I had slain thee, and saved her alive' (Num 22:32–33). Balaam submits and proposes to turn back. Second volte-face: the Angel of the Lord tells him to continue on his way: 'Go with the men: but only the word that I shall speak unto thee, that thou shalt speak' (Num 22:35).

Balaam as parodic double of Moses. We have the night and the divine command to depart. And we have the second thoughts of the Lord: he sent Moses on a mission and then threatened to kill him; he seems to want Balaam to leave, and then no longer to want it, and then to want it again. We also have the same divine ambush: the Angel who attacks the prophet. And the unarmed prophet who sees nothing, understands nothing, does nothing, cannot do anything. The same physical wound is present, which is minor, however, and inglorious: Balaam's crushed foot for Eliezer's circumcised member . . . Moses's donkey has become a she-ass, to which Zipporah's role has bizarrely fallen: that of saving the prophet from impending death. In the wake of Balaam's story, there will even be some Midianite women. But, while the Midianite wife of Moses, Zipporah, distinguished herself by carrying out a command of the Law (circumcision), those who appear on this occasion are vectors of the worst of transgressions: it is they who, with the women of Moab, incite Israel to wallow in lust and idolatry in Shittim. They and their people will be severely punished, by order of God addressed to Moses himself.

Balaam as caricature of Moses. His story is basically ridiculous, with multiple twists, and garrulous. Everyone in it goes on at length, opportunely or inopportunely, even the she-ass. Who can be surprised that God should toy with this man – this derisory magician, perverse adviser, prophet *malgré lui*? Who will take offence if he sends him an angel who suddenly looms up before Balaam as an 'obstacle', an 'adversary', I dare not say as 'Satan'?[10] Balaam is not a righteous man. God does not put him to the test. He abuses and humiliates him. And he mocks him, obliging him to bless – not once but thrice – where he intended to curse. The case of Balaam – a rogue imitation of the first of the prophets – does not explain that of Moses. Quite the reverse. What is understandable and justifiable in the former case becomes incomprehensible, unjustifiable, in the latter. Far from solving the mystery, the parallel exacerbates it. It underscores the extraordinary brutality of the fate imposed on Moses, all of it dispatched in three verses: a fate which, to be understood and (perhaps) justified, requires further comparisons.

Rashi and, before him, some of his sources point us in the right direction. When Balaam rose in the morning, and saddled his ass before setting off, God supposedly called out: 'Wicked man! Abraham, their father, has already preceded you!' – accusing him of imitating, in vain and with bad intentions, a deed previously performed for good by the ancestral patriarch of the Hebrews. Further on, according to the same sources, when he discovers that God does not authorize (or no longer authorizes) his journey, and that his angel is blocking the path, Balaam allegedly exclaims: 'It is [God] himself who ordered me to set off and you, angel, are retracting his words! Such is his habit: he says one thing and sends his angel to go back on it! He said to Abraham: "Take now thy son . . ." (Gen 22:2) and, via an angel, retracted his words!' Balaam is not only the rogue double of Moses, he is also the rogue double of the founder of the line of Israel. Abraham has already experienced what Moses is experiencing before our eyes. But that is definitely not all. There is a further step to be taken. There is another precedent for Moses's ordeal: that inflicted on another patriarch, Jacob. Abraham, Jacob and Moses: a trinity of similarly tried righteous men. Balaam is a caricature of all three.

It is for these three – three righteous men – that journeys and/or night are the time of trial, truth and possible death. Moses has saddled his donkey and set off, with wife and children, obeying the call of the Lord: 'Go, return into Egypt' (Exod 4:19). Before him, Abraham too had one day saddled his donkey and set off, with Isaac and his two servants, obeying the summons of the Lord: 'Get thee into the land of Moriah; and offer him [your son Isaac] there for a burnt offering upon one of the mountains which I will tell thee of' (Gen 22:2). Before Moses, and after Abraham, Jacob too, who would one night have to wrestle with the Angel, had set off, with wives and children, obeying the Lord's summons: 'Return unto the land of thy fathers, and to thy kindred; and I will be with thee' (Gen 31:3).

In each instance, the ordeal takes place on the road: Moses is approached by the Lord, who seeks to kill him; Abraham must put to death the person dearest to him; and Jacob wrestles with the Angel 'until the breaking of the day' (Gen 32:24). In two cases (Moses and Abraham), everything seems to revolve around a son (Eliezer, the circumcised son, and Isaac, the son intended for the sacrifice). In two cases, the ordeal precedes a meeting with a brother: returning to Egypt, Moses will meet again with Aaron, his deputy; returning to Canaan, Jacob will meet again with Esau, his rival. In each case, the ordeal is survived: the Lord 'releases' Moses; an 'angel of the Lord' stays Abraham's arm as he

is about to sacrifice Isaac; Jacob is not vanquished by the mysterious nocturnal opponent.

God desired Moses's death (or would have us believe he did)
and it is the sacrifice of his son's foreskin that saved him. God
desired the death of Abraham's son (or would have him believe
he did) and in the end Abraham sacrificed a ram instead of his
son. And it was a 'man' (an angel? God himself?) who confronted
Jacob and, unable to vanquish him, spared him, after having
'pressed', 'wounded', or simply 'touched'[11] his thigh. Each time,
the key thing is what is called into question – and by God
himself: Moses's mission, Abraham's posterity, and Jacob the
father of the tribes of Israel. If God (or his messenger) satisfies
his desire, real or affected; if God does not stop; or if nothing
stops him, everything comes to a stop. It is his own, those closest
to him, whom God subjects to the worst of ordeals. And he can,
at any moment, rescind (or seem to rescind) his own plans. It is
cruel, it is absurd, but that is how it is. We have got to accept it.
Or not. Insurmountable darkness of God. Job will feel less alone.

When all is said and done, however, something still resists
comparison. There is something undeniably unique about our
three verses of darkness and terror.

The extraordinarily condensed character of the text: three
verses, that's all.

And the extra character: a woman. This woman is Zipporah.
Moses met her by a well, married her, had two children with her.
She will play no further role in the biblical story. These three verses
of darkness and terror are *the* moment – the sole moment – of
Zipporah. In it she is a mother (of the son she circumcises) and a
wife (of the husband she thereby saves). But she is more than that.

Of the four characters in the plot, only two are active: God,
who targets Moses, and Zipporah, who saves Moses from

God's hands. It is she who confronts God, no one else. The circumcised infant is obviously passive. And Moses is passive too, especially so: it is perhaps the only point in his story where he can do nothing – does nothing. Zipporah, by contrast, acts. She acts like a man, performing a male act (circumcision) on the male member (of her son), thereby saving another man (her husband) and, in so doing, saving the mission entrusted to him. Finally, Zipporah speaks and even speaks twice. Here the power to act, and the power to speak, are hers and hers alone.

Abraham held out. Jacob fought. Moses is altogether destroyed; he is no longer anything. Nothing more than the stake, the victim, in a contest that surpasses him. Moses is no longer a prophet. God does not speak to him. He does not speak to God. At no time does God reveal his intentions – not even to the reader. There is not the least explanatory verse for him, as there was for Abraham: 'And it came to pass after these things, that God did tempt Abraham' (Gen 22:1). Nothing prior to the ordeal, then, to announce it as such. And nothing afterwards either: (the Angel of) God will not speak to him, will not change his name, will not bless him, as he did in the case of Jacob. And Moses, of whom it would be said after his death that he had been (and remained) a peerless prophet whom God had known and communicated with 'face to face' (Deut 34:10), this Moses will not say on the threshold of his mission, as did Jacob after his ordeal: 'I have seen God face to face, and my life is preserved' (Gen 32:30).

In these pure instants of terror and darkness, Moses is definitively silent and utterly fragile. Moses whose salvation depends completely on a woman, a foreign woman, who alone possesses the key and the meaning of the ordeal he undergoes and from which she saves him.

4

A Woman Called Moses

Those who are absent are always wrong. And, sometimes, it is not a good idea to dawdle at the top of mountains – even when it is for excellent reasons, detained by an Interlocutor whom one evades at one's peril. At the very moment when, at the end of their long interview, the Lord consigns the two stone tablets engraved by his finger to Moses, anxiety and impatience suddenly grip a people who feel abandoned by their God and their leader alike.

The affair of the Golden Calf has begun. Aaron gives in to the pleas of his flock, supplying a miserable substitute god and leader for their perverse devotion. The fragment of a verse that introduces the account of this affair is very brief – six short words in Hebrew and not many more in translation: 'The people saw that Moses delayed to come down' (Exod 32:1). It seems all the shorter given that it is supposed to explain – I dare not say justify – the most dramatic episode recounted by the Pentateuch: an act of wholesale betrayal by Israel on the very morrow of the Exodus and the theophany of Sinai.

Short, and somewhat obscure. For a start, what does it mean to 'see' a delay? A delay is not 'seen', but estimated, calculated. Next, why should Israel think that Moses 'delayed'? Did it know when he was supposed to descend from his mountain? Yes, it did; according to Rashi and some of his sources, Israel knew, or at least thought it did. And it may well have been the victim both of an error of calculation and of a diabolical trap.

The error of calculation, to start with. Moses had announced that he would return after forty days, before the end of the sixth hour. By that he meant forty full days, each including a night and a day.[1] Now, Moses began his ascent very early in the morning of 7 *sivan*.[2] That day should therefore not have counted. The Hebrews had overlooked this, and so expected Moses to return on the 16th of the following month (*tammuz*) – not the 17th.[3] On the 16th, misled by their miscalculation, not seeing Moses descend, they thought that he was late. A question then inevitably arose: what was the cause of this delay?

And here, as is to be expected, Satan intervenes. Imagining a delay is one thing; interpreting it is quite another. If Moses is late, it is quite simply because he is dead. In the biblical text, the Hebrews address Aaron in these terms: 'Moses, the man that brought us up out of the land of Egypt, we wot not what is become of him' (Exod 32:1). But this is just a manner of speaking, a euphemism. In fact, they know – or think they know. At least Satan leads them to think they do, insinuating himself diabolically into their hearts, as suggested by a Targum:[4]

The people saw that Moses delayed to come down out of the mount, [and] the people gathered themselves together unto Aaron, *when they saw that the time Moses had fixed had passed. Then Satan came to pervert them and their hearts grew proud* and [the people] said unto [Aaron], Up, make us gods, which shall go before us; for as for this Moses, the man that brought us up out of the land of Egypt, *he has been consumed by flames on the mountain in a blazing fire before the Lord*. We wot not what is become of him.[5]

This scenario is not unappealing. And the suggestion Satan plants in the mind of the Hebrews is logical enough: such familiarity with divine fire is to risk being consumed by it . . . Nevertheless, Rashi and some of his sources prefer a more spectacular production to this minimalist scenario. On that famous 16 *sivan*, when the Hebrews already think that Moses is late, Satan pulls out all the stops. He sows confusion across the world, causes an appearance of darkness and disorder to prevail, so that a single explanation of Moses's lateness naturally dictates itself: the cause of such upheavals can only be the prophet's death. And Satan personally confirms it: 'Yes, Moses is dead, six hours have already passed,[6] and he has not returned.' Intent on winning the Hebrews' unreserved support, he pushes manipulation further still. Satan not only displays confusion and darkness to them, but also the dead Moses himself! Or at least a simulacrum of his coffin traversing the celestial sphere.[7]

So it is not Moses's delay that impels the Hebrews to disavowal, but his death, or apparent death. The scenario conceived by Satan recalls another – the death of Jesus himself:

And it was about the *sixth hour*, and there was a *darkness over all the earth* until the ninth hour. And the sun was darkened, and the veil of the temple was rent in the midst. And when Jesus had cried with a loud voice, he said, Father, into thy

hands I commend my spirit: and having said thus, he gave up
the ghost (Luke 23:44–6).

Deep down, is the simulacrum of Moses's death and the ascension of his dead body to Heaven, as evoked by rabbinical sources
glossing Exodus 32:1, not a parody of Jesus' death and ascension,
assuming a polemical dimension and, above all, prompting a
reading of Jesus's death and ascension as themselves simulacra? If
Satan is manoeuvring in one instance, he must be in the other,
too. And, if Moses's fake death propels the Hebrews into idolatry
of the Golden Calf, is it not into another form of idolatry –
Christianity – that the genuine death (and fake resurrection) of
Jesus propel his followers? Should the fabrication and worship
of the Golden Calf be seen as an image or prefiguration of the
future emergence of the Nazarene heresy?

Very likely. But we cannot stop there. The scenario – at once
theatrical, ironic, derisory and critical – sketched by some
Midrashic commentators on the basis of Exodus 32 may play
more than a polemical, potentially anti-Christian, role. Visually,
and in the mode of sinister farce, it dramatizes a theme that in a
completely different way runs through the whole biblical account
of the episode of the Golden Calf. It functions as a falsely
grotesque hook and actually draws attention to the key thing,
even as it seems to deflect from it. The key thing? Moses's very
status and (let us venture the formula) his possible Christic
dimension.

Moses the Intercessor
The infidelity of the Golden Calf episode radically alters God's
relationship to his people. All of a sudden, Israel is no longer
simply the Lord's people. When it sins grievously, it becomes

Moses's people: 'And the Lord said unto Moses, Go, get thee down; for thy people, which thou broughtest out of the land of Egypt, have corrupted themselves' (Exod 32:7).

According to an old rabbinical tradition, it is not to Israel in the strict sense – the descendants of the Patriarchs – that God is referring here, but to the crowd of foreigners who attached themselves to the Hebrews at the time of the exodus and whom Moses, happy to attract new recruits under the wing of the divine Presence, agreed to convert without even informing God. It was these new converts, poorly Judaized and still steeped in idolatrous practices and beliefs, who were corrupted and in turn corrupted the Lord's people. This would certainly be very convenient and, at least in part, exculpate the Israel of blood lineage – the true inheritor of divine promises – from the worst transgression in its history.

Moreover, when God says to Moses 'Go, get thee down', according to the same traditions he did not simply mean 'descend' from the mountain to check out what is happening below, and try to restore order. For Moses, this descent is a veritable demotion, with God telling him: 'Descend from your greatness!' Because Moses's greatness was granted to him only in connection with the people he was supposed to lead on the path of obedience. The people's fault is, in the first instance, the prophet's: 'At this point', says Rashi, 'Moses was excommunicated by decree of the celestial Tribunal.'

Yet the sequel to the story seems to point up the rather dubious character of such speculation. After all, God's anger is unsparing and has no time for subtle distinctions. It is indeed 'this people' – the people as a whole – whom God accuses of being 'stiffnecked' (Exod 32:9), 'this people' in its entirety whom he intends to punish, in the most radical way: 'let . . . my wrath . . . wax hot against them, [so] that I may consume them' (Exod 32:10). In addition, Moses does not appear to be relieved of his original title at all. On the contrary. Curiously, even though the prophet has not yet said anything, God asks him to cease protesting: 'Now, therefore let me alone, that my wrath may wax hot against them', and so on. In so doing, he 'opens a door' to his prophet and intimates that everything may depend on him; that his intercession, his prayers, might have the power to annul the divine decree. He even incites him, through hints, to speak up in defence of his people. Has Moses really 'descended from greatness'? No, especially given that, after stating his intention to destroy Israel, God makes him an astonishing proposal: 'let . . . my wrath wax hot against them, [so] that I may consume them: and I will make of thee a great nation' (Exod 32:10).

Clean slate, fresh start. We are already familiar with this. In the Flood, God wiped the whole of perverted humanity off the face of the Earth and assigned to Noah and his descendants sole responsibility for starting again from scratch. The God who creates is also the one who destroys. But the God who promises is also bound by his promises. Here, he confronts Moses with a choice, a challenge. He compels him, as it were, to define his role and status precisely and definitively. Either he will be Moses, the man who prays, intercedes and reminds God of his promises, thereby saving a nation of sinners and ensuring the continuity of its history. Or he will be like a second Noah, the man of a new start; like a new Abraham, the forebear of a new line.

Moses does not expressly respond to the second proposal. He nonetheless clearly rejects it, sticking to his role of interceding prophet. He re-establishes Israel as God's people: 'Lord, why doth thy wrath wax hot against *thy* people, which *thou* hast brought forth out of the land of Egypt with great power, and with a mighty hand?' (Exod 32:11). He reminds God of the duties incumbent on him by virtue of his grandeur in the eyes of all nations: 'Wherefore should the Egyptians speak, and say, For mischief did he bring them out, to slay them in the mountains, and to consume them from the face of the earth?' (Exod 32:12). Finally, he urges God to honour his previous commitments: 'Remember Abraham, Isaac, and Israel, thy servants, to whom thou swarest by thine own self, and saidst unto them, I will multiply your seed as the stars of heaven, and all this land that I have spoken of will I give unto your seed, and they shall inherit it for ever' (Exod 32:13).

Moses will not be a new Abraham: he will instead be the guarantor of respect for the promises made to Abraham and his descendants. And, according to some traditions, it is precisely the invocation of the Patriarchs' merits that enables him to save their descendants from destruction: 'If [the Hebrews] deserve death by fire' (Moses supposedly said), 'remember Abraham who was ready to die for you by fire in Ur Kasdim!⁸ If they deserve death by the sword, remember Isaac who stretched out his neck during the sacrifice on Mount Moriah!⁹ If they deserve exile, remember Jacob, who was exiled to Haran!'¹⁰ Moses may even have added: 'And if the merit of these three is insufficient to save them, how can you say to me [who am alone]: "I will make of thee a great nation"?'

It is tempting to say that, by negotiating and arguing thus, Moses follows in the footsteps of Abraham himself – the patriarch who similarly sought to make God spare the inhabitants of Sodom, doomed to destruction. However, it would be a mistake. Abraham employed an absolute, universal ethical argument against God: 'Will thou also destroy the righteous with the wicked?' (Gen 18:23). Moses, for his part, invokes the sight of the nations, the merit of the Fathers, the promises that have been made to them. Abraham fails: God agrees to spare the city if he can find ten righteous men in it, but their dialogue is interrupted, and Sodom is ultimately destroyed. Moses ends up obtaining forgiveness for his people.

But if he seems – only seems – greater than Abraham, Moses is such because he has Abraham with him; because he can rely on him and his merit. In a sense, Moses is powerful solely in and through the power conferred on him by Abraham. And he himself renounces being a new Abraham, the ancestor of a new line. He does not hope for any promise for himself; he merely aspires to see the promise made to Abraham kept. Moses is simply Moses: one who intercedes, reminds and prays. This is a fundamental aspect of Moses's humility – a humility that accounts for his greatness; that enables him to obtain God's repentance and thus, paradoxically, more than Abraham was ever able to obtain. Sodom was destroyed despite Abraham. Israel will be saved thanks to Moses.

While not being as great as Abraham – though that is precisely where his greatness lies – Moses is definitely greater than Noah. Because he is righteous, Noah is saved from the waters of the Flood. At no stage does he intercede for anyone. He obeys: 'according to all that God commanded him, so did he' (Gen 6:22). God tells him to save himself and he saves himself. God announces that he will seal a covenant with him and he accepts this covenant. God tells him: 'The end of all flesh is come before me' (Gen 6:13), and this too he accepts. 'And it repented [*va-yin-nahem*] the Lord that he had made man on the earth' (Gen 6:6): Noah is fine with it. He complies with this creative God who turns into a destructive God. Moses does quite the opposite: he does not obey, but intercedes; he does not seek to save himself, but to save his people; he hears God's judgement, but rejects it; he does not hope for any new covenant for himself or his descendants, but fights tooth and nail to get the destructive God to renounce destruction. And he succeeds: 'And the Lord repented [*va-yinnahem*] of the evil which he thought to do unto his people' (Exod 32:14).

'Blot Me Out!'

However, the story does not end there. And the continuation is, frankly, rather confusing. The people are not destroyed, but they are punished. On at least three occasions. First by Moses, who makes them drink water mixed with the dust of the idol, after having ground it to powder (thus condemning the culprits, Rashi tells us, to a lethal form of dropsy). Once again by Moses, who launches the sons of Levi upon a bloody punitive expedition, with 3,000 men being put to the sword. Finally, by God himself: 'And the Lord plagued the people, because they made the calf, which Aaron made' (Exod 32:35) – death by epidemic this time, Rashi informs us.

The situation again seems so critical that Moses intervenes once more: 'And now I will go up unto the Lord; peradventure I shall make an atonement for your sin' (Exod 32:30). The formula is ambiguous and does not really indicate what Moses intends to do. One thing is clear, however: this time it is no longer a question of reminding God of his promises and obliging him to keep them, but of treating Israel's offence directly, negotiating its erasure, and getting the Lord to regard it henceforth as expiated. The strategy developed by Moses in these circumstances is fundamentally different from the one he employed earlier. Phase one, he acknowledges the extreme gravity of the transgression: 'Oh, this people have sinned a great sin, and have made them gods of gold' (Exod 32:31). Phase two, he begs forgiveness: 'Yet now, if thou wilt forgive their sin . . .' (Exod 32:32). Phase three, he throws all his own weight into the balance: 'and if not, blot me out, I pray thee, out of thy book which thou hast written' (Exod 32:32).

An astonishing piece of blackmail? Staggering presumption on the prophet's part? Or an ultimate expression of the most profound despondency? Before deciding, assuming we have to choose, we need to clarify Moses's intention, the exact meaning of the words he uses.

'Blot me out': the expression is powerful, brutal, suggesting a radical measure. What is usually blotted out in Hebrew? Sometimes sin: 'I have blotted out, as a thick cloud, thy transgressions, and, as a cloud, thy sins' (Is 44:22). More often the sinner himself. Thus, the perverted creatures of Noah's time, drowned in the Flood: 'and every living substance that I have made will I blot out from off the face of the earth' (Gen 7:4). Similarly, later, Amalek, the irreducible and emblematic enemy of Israel, who can be forgiven nothing; Amalek who, not fearing God, attacked the Hebrews from behind, targeting the laggards and a whole exhausted people that had just escaped slavery: 'Thou shalt blot out the remembrance of Amalek from under heaven; thou shalt not forget it' (Deut 25:19).

The sinner, his name, even his memory are blotted out. At least, a wish to do so is expressed. And the formula will remain, condensed, uttered as a curse against any absolute wrongdoer, irrevocably condemned to destruction and oblivion: *Yimmah shemo ve-zikhro!* Let his name and memory be blotted out! Jesus will figure among the cursed, obviously, he whose name[11] is traditionally interpreted in the Jewish world not as a name, but as the opposite of a name, as a name that is already the erasure of a name, the three letters that supposedly compose it being nothing other than the initials of the three words of the dreaded formula.[12] Is this what Moses asks for himself? That he, the righteous one, should be purely and simply blotted out like the worst of sinners?

In truth, Moses's request is at once more precise and vaguer. What he asks of God, should the latter refuse Israel forgiveness, is to be 'blot[ted] . . . out of thy book which thou hast written' (Exod 32:32). But which 'book' written by God? And what does it mean to be 'blotted out'? For Rashi and others, the matter is clear: Moses demands nothing less than to be blotted out 'of the whole Torah'. Why? 'So that it is not said of me that I was incapable of asking mercy for them'.[13] The Torah without the name of Moses, the Torah without Moses? Hard to imagine. Besides, how could anything be 'blotted' from a book that in fact, at the time Moses is speaking, has not yet been written? Finally, if the 'book' referred to by Moses is indeed the Torah, how are we to take God's response to him: 'Whosoever hath sinned against me, him I will blot out of my book' (Exod 32:33)? The Torah, as we know, is not silent on the names of sinners – quite the reverse. It must therefore be another 'book' that God and Moses are referring to here. The book of Heavenly Decrees? Or, more simply, the 'Book of Life'? Moses would then be asking to be erased from the 'Book of the Living'. In a word, in the event of God refusing Israel his forgiveness, does Moses simply ask to die?

In other circumstances, containing echoes of these, Moses speaks more clearly. Thus, in Chapter 11 of the Book of Numbers, the Hebrews have had enough of manna; they want meat and complain restlessly, 'every man in the door of his tent' (Num 11:10). God grows extremely angry. This new ordeal

affects Moses profoundly. He cannot stand it: it is too burdensome. He expressly begs to die: 'Kill me, I pray thee, out of
hand, if I have found favour in thy sight; and let me not see my
wretchedness' (Num 11:15). For some commentators, the 'blot
me . . . out of thy book' of Exodus 32:32 has no other meaning
than the 'kill me' here. But if discouragement moves Moses to
desire death in the episode in Numbers, what inspires the same
wish in the episode of the Golden Calf? What does Moses's
aspiration to self-erasure mean there? And what exactly is the
link that unites this aspiration to the issue of forgiveness for
Israel? Does Moses want to die so as not to witness God refuse
Israel his pardon, and not see his name associated with that
refusal? Or, by his own death, by his self-sacrifice, does he hope
to obtain forgiveness for Israel?

Christian Moses

Moses Nachmanides* puts it plainly. What Moses offers God is
a deal: 'Yet now, if thou wilt forgive their sin, *it will be the result
of thy mercy*; and if not, blot me *in their stead* . . . [from the]
book *of life, and it is I who will endure the punishment intended
for them*.'[14]

In this respect, Moses simply forms part of a venerable tradition. Patriarchs and prophets have always been quick to offer
themselves as a sacrifice in place of their flock. Like Jonah asking
to be cast into the sea to save the boat he is on, which is threatened by a violent storm (Jon 1:12), or like David asking God to
divert the calamity striking the people onto him and his family
(II Sam 24:17), Moses offers himself up to God's wrath to spare
the Hebrews from the disaster befalling them.[15] However, the
comparison is misleading or, at best, inexact. In fact, if the storm
threatens to destroy Jonah's vessel, it is because Jonah has sinned,

by running away from the mission God wanted to entrust to him. Similarly, if Israel is struck by the plague, it is because David has sinned, by ordering a census against God's will. What has Moses done for Israel to incur the epidemic that is already afflicting it, or threatens to? Moses has done nothing, he has not sinned. It is Israel that has sinned by worshipping the Golden Calf. Moses does not simply ask to undergo in lieu of Israel the disaster about to strike it. He asks to bear its sin and be punished in its place: 'blot me *in their stead* from the book *of life, and it is I who will endure the punishment intended for them.*'

To clarify the precise nature of Moses's suggestion, Nachmanides hits upon this verse from Isaiah: 'As is said in Scripture [Isa 53:5], "he was wounded for our transgressions, he was bruised for our iniquities: the chastisement of our peace was upon him; and with his stripes we are healed."' What Nachmanides tells us indirectly here is that Moses attempted before God to assume the role of the suffering Servant evoked in Isaiah 53. As is well known, this passage is the object of a lively exegetical battle between Judaism and Christianity. Who is this Servant of the Lord? The future Messiah? Israel itself as a collective, presented in the guise of an individual, suffering among pagans for the world's salvation? Or is it, as Christians argue, Jesus, the Messiah who has already come? Naturally, I shall not venture to pronounce on this point. What matters to me is that Moses himself might well have been tempted to fit into this mould. Nachmanides is neither the first, nor the last, to suggest it. A Talmudic tradition thus establishes differently an explicit link between the episode we are concerned with and the suffering Servant depicted in Isaiah. Like the suffering Servant to come, Rabbi Simlai (second half of the third century) tells us, Moses 'poured out his soul unto death' (Isa 53:12) when he said,

'Blot me' (Exod 32:32). Like the suffering Servant to come, Moses only 'bore [or tried to bear?] the sin of many' (Isa 53:12), when he sought to obtain expiation for the sin of the Golden Calf (and partially succeeded).

Yet the offence of the Golden Calf is to Israel rather what 'original sin' is to Christians. At least if we are to believe an old Talmudic adage,[16] echoed by Rashi, according to which 'no punishment comes upon Israel without it containing part payment for the sin of the Golden Calf.' And this is how we are to understand what God himself says at the very end of his exchange with Moses. Eventually agreeing not to destroy all the children of Israel for the offence they have just committed, the Lord does not renounce punishing them for it in part every time he punishes them for other sins in the future: 'in the day when I visit [*other sins upon them*] I will [*also*] visit their sin [*of the Golden Calf*] upon them' (Exod 32:34). This 'original' sin of Israel's is at the heart of the request made by Moses. And such is the choice he dares to put to his interlocutor: either God, by virtue of his mercy, simply grants forgiveness, or he accepts the death of Moses as an expiatory sacrifice.

Moses trades one erasure for another: his own in return for erasure of his people's sin. He trades one annihilation for another: his own in return, and as compensation, for the non-annihilation of his people. He who, but a few verses earlier, out of the modesty that is his true greatness, refused, implicitly at any rate, to become a second Abraham and/or a new Noah, reckons he can count for as much as the whole of Israel and even a bit more. He agrees to bear the sin of a whole people alone – a sin with which he has not in any way been associated. He takes it as given, or at least possible, that the sacrifice of a single righteous man is enough to expiate the sin of a whole people and ensure its salvation. Moses's aspiration to self-erasure ('Blot me!'), far from being only, or merely, the ultimate expression of his humility, is perhaps above all an aspiration to absolute greatness. It raises the question of the possible access of the greatest of prophets to a specifically messianic and Christic dimension. Moses wishes to assume the role of Isaiah's suffering Servant. Will he do so in the end?

The very first verse to evoke the figure of the Servant of the Lord in the Book of Isaiah stresses his greatness: 'my servant . . . shall be exalted and extolled, and be very high' (Isa 52:13). A Midrashic tradition, reported by Nachmanides in his commentary on this verse, clarifies the meaning of the repetition: 'He [the Messiah] will be exalted above Abraham, he will be extolled over Moses, he will be situated higher than the angels of Service.' Whatever meaning we attribute to this teaching, it is clear, according to him, that Moses – like Abraham and even the angels – remains below, or beneath, messianic dignity. What is suggested by this Midrashic tradition is affirmed by God himself in his own way, indirectly and abruptly, in the Book of Exodus: 'Whosoever hath sinned against me, him will I blot out of my book' (Exod 32:33).

This verdict – biblical rather than Midrashic, divine rather than exegetical – is clear and beyond appeal. I do not know if it applies beyond Moses – that is, whether it is the definitive expression of a general, absolute principle, according to which no one (no human being whatever) can be punished for the sin of another (a fortiori of an entire people) and obtain forgiveness for him by paying the penalty in his stead. What I do know, though, is that it applies to Moses; and that it reduces Moses to his primary, non-transcendable humanity. However great a prophet, however righteous in all his acts, there is something Moses cannot obtain: for his self-sacrifice to count as expiation of Israel's 'original' sin.

Moses is, can be, and must be nothing but a humble intercessor. His prayer, it will be remembered, his sole prayer – merely a reminder to God of his promises – and his fully assumed modesty – refusing to be the father of a new holy line – pulled God back from the pure and simple annihilation of the initial sentence: 'And the Lord repented *(va-yinnahem)* of the evil which he thought to do unto his people' (Exod 32:14). By contrast, the offer of his own sacrifice, the ultimate claim to excessive grandeur, remains ineffectual, or almost:

> And the Lord said unto Moses, Whosoever hath sinned against me, him will I blot out of my book. Therefore now go, lead the people unto the place of which I have spoken unto thee: behold, mine Angel shall go before thee: nevertheless in the day when I visit I will visit their sin upon them. And the Lord plagued the people, because they made the calf, which Aaron made (Exod 32:33–5).

What did Moses gain by offering himself as an expiatory victim? Cancellation of the punishment? Not at all. At best, postponement, its enactment being staggered. Israel will not pay its debt in full, straight away, by its complete destruction. But it will pay, day after day, over time. God himself withdraws and it is an 'angel' who will henceforth go before Israel in its trek. As for Moses, God calls him sharply to order and puts him in his rightful place. Moses will not be the Christ of Israel, merely the man assigned by God to lead Israel where God wishes him to lead it. Is this a humiliation of Moses? No. Simply a reminder of his frail humanity. Moses is still one among the Hebrews (even if he is the best of them).

Virile Moses

Is Moses fully human? He is rather fully a man – which is not quite the same thing. The virility of Moses is fragile, for sure, haunted by a desire for death and tempted by renunciation, but it is virility all the same. 'The man Moses' is also that. This is what Scripture makes us see first. And, like it or not, it is what continues to haunt our imaginaries. Moses is a man, nothing more than a man, and when he momentarily dreams of realizing himself as the Christ of Israel, it is God himself who reminds him of his limits. The essentially human limits of an unsurpassably human potential. This is what makes him 'one of the Hebrews', 'one of us'. But say what they may, this means – pending further information – one of us *men*. Can we de-masculinize Moses? Some challenge. And if it were possible, would that suffice to feminize him?

It is true that Moses's world is not a male world through and through. This is not saying much, but it's something. He has two sons, of course, borne him by Zipporah. But he does not place his hopes in them – far from it. In this, at any rate, he is no ordinary father and perhaps not a father at all. Nor is he really much of a husband. If we believe tradition,[17] he rapidly decided to impose total sexual abstinence on himself, believing that the intimacy and continuity of his relations with the divine Presence demanded extra purity.[18] Moreover, Moses proves attentive to the petitions of women themselves. Thus, he benevolently receives the daughters of Zelophehad, come to claim the inheritance of their father, who died without leaving a son. Consulted by Moses, God will grant this request (Num 27:1–11).

There is more. Women play a central, crucial role in Moses's destiny – a vital one even, in the precise sense of the word. His biological mother, Jochebed, gives birth to him, hides him for three months and, by so doing, saves his life for the first time.

Granted, she then abandons him, only for the reins to be taken up by another woman – sister Miriam, who watches over the baby basket drifting on the Nile. Finally, along comes Pharaoh's daughter, to rescue the infant from the waters. Miriam intervenes once again and suggests to Pharaoh's daughter that she take on Jochebed as a wet nurse. By this point, the three women have combined to ensure the best for Moses. Later, yet another woman will save him: wife Zipporah, who will circumcise their son during a very dark night, compelling the Angel of Death to release his grip on the prophet. So far, so good, though somewhat ambiguous: Jochebed, the biological mother, does abandon Moses; Pharaoh's daughter, the adoptive mother, abruptly and terminally disappears from the narrative; Miriam herself ends up maligning her brother – on account of another woman, what's more, whom Moses had married – and will be punished for it (Num 12);[19] as for Zipporah, she will be repudiated by Moses and will in turn disappear from the story. Only for a moment does Moses depend on the women around him. In addition to the fact that his relations with them remain ambivalent, their presence and role in no way alter the androcentric character of the narrative, focused on 'the man Moses', and do not significantly dilute the man's irreducible, dominant masculinity. On the contrary, indeed.

So, is a feminine Moses a mere chimera? Despite everything, perhaps not. One episode, mentioned earlier, opens the gap we thought we were seeking in vain. It will reveal to us a Moses who is fully a man because he is also a woman.

'Like a Woman'

It is a familiar story: dissatisfied and ungrateful, the people complain and rebel, God threatens, and Moses has to handle it. All of a sudden, Egypt appears to its former slaves as a lost culinary paradise: 'Who shall give us flesh to eat? We remember the fish, which we did eat in Egypt freely; the cucumbers, and the melons, and the leeks, and the onions, and the garlick: But now our soul is dried away: there is nothing at all, beside this manna, before our eyes' (Num 11:4–6). God has a furious outburst and Moses is filled with sadness. This time, however, he cracks. The problem is meat, obviously. Where is he to find any meat in this arid desert? But that is not all. For the problem is also, perhaps most of all, the crushing responsibility God has imposed on his servant: 'the burden of all this people' (Num 11:11). Moses asks for one thing: not meat, but deliverance from this burden. He resigns: 'I am not able to bear all this people alone, because it is too heavy for me' (Num 11:14). He prefers death to such a life: 'Kill me, I pray thee, out of hand, if I have found favour in thy sight' (Num 11:15).

Why, exactly, does Moses want to die? In order to 'not see my wretchedness', he says (Num 11:15). But what exactly is his wretchedness in this instance? The first possibility is that it is the wretchedness occasioned by the interminable complaints of an unruly people, the simple misery of the burden imposed on him. But the second possibility is that it is the wretchedness Israel itself will endure at the end of this latest bout of insurgency. For Israel will have meat: it will eat quails, it will be sated and even nauseated by overeating. But then it will be punished: the Lord's ire will explode against it, he will smite it 'with a very great plague' (Num 11:33). Perhaps this is what Moses does not wish to see (and which, as a good prophet, he foresees). He does not have the strength; he prefers dying to witnessing the wretchedness of his people, which is also his.

Whichever alternative we opt for, the nature of the death wish expressed by Moses does not change. We are not dealing with a repeat of the incident of the Golden Calf. There is no self-sacrifice here. Moses is not trying to spare Israel anything. He simply wishes not to see. And what he requests is the plain and stark deliverance that is death. It is as if the greatest of prophets has vanished. Just a man remains. A man at the end of his tether. Not even a man. Or more than a man. A woman, in fact. Simple as that.

Let us review Moses's complaint in full:

> Wherefore hast thou afflicted thy servant? and wherefore have I not found favour in thy sight, that thou layest the burden of all this people upon me? Have I *conceived* all this people? have I *begotten* them, that thou shouldest say unto me, Carry them in thy *bosom*, as a [*nurse*] beareth the *sucking child*, unto the land which thou swarest unto their fathers? Whence should I have flesh to give unto all this people? for they weep unto me, saying, Give us flesh, that we may eat. I am not able to bear all this people alone, because it is too heavy for me. And if thou deal thus with me, kill me, I pray thee, out of hand, if I have found favour in thy sight; and let me not see my wretchedness (Num 11:11–15).

Moses rejects Israel like an infant that is not his or not initially, or not only, his, and for whom he cannot take responsibility, like a suckling child demanding its pittance but whom he is unable to feed. Everything is in the masculine, obviously, but the role that is so burdensome to Moses, which God has forced on him, and which he feels incapable of performing, manifestly possesses all the attributes of a maternal role. So, was it Moses who conceived this people? He who bore it? Does God have the right to ask him to carry it in his bosom, 'as a [nurse] beareth the suckling child'? But, by the way, are we so sure that it is the refusal to be a mother which inspires Moses's long, poignant lament to God? Is it not rather a refusal to shoulder the role *alone* ('I am not able to bear all this people alone')? Is the complaint not also a reproach to God for offloading onto Moses a responsibility that is primarily his? Is not Israel God's first-born?[20] Is the complaint not also a criticism of God for making it so difficult for him to fully assume the role of mother imposed on him? And perhaps an advance reproof for imminently inflicting on him the spectacle of the calamity, the terrible punishment, that is going to befall his child?

A woman called Moses: she is here. Rashi and his supercommentator, Elijah Mizrachi*, confirm it for us, basing themselves on a rigorous analysis of the formula used by the prophet to justify his death wish: '*And if thou deal thus with me*, kill me, I pray thee, out of hand' (Num 11:15). In Hebrew, *ve-im kakhah at oseh li*. Let us translate word by word. *Ve-im*: and-if. *Kakhah*: thus. *At*: you. *Oseh*: do. *Li*: to-me. So, literally: 'and-if thus you do to-me'. The problem, however, is that what seems to be the subject of the verb – *at* (you) – is a feminine pronoun in Hebrew (something neither French nor English can convey), whereas the verb is in the masculine (likewise impossible to convey in French or English). Supposing that the editor of the biblical text cannot have been a bad grammarian, Rashi and Mizrachi suggest: (1) that 'you' (in the feminine) cannot be the subject of the verb (in the masculine); (2) that 'you' (in the feminine) obviously cannot refer to God; (3) that the actual subject of the verb is indeed God, but that this subject is omitted or understood; (4) that 'you' (in the feminine), not being able to refer to God, can in fact refer only to Moses. This leads them to construe the fragment of verse thus: 'And-if thus, [*you*] make of-me [*a feminine*] "you"';

and leads us to retranslate Moses's apostrophe as follows: 'And if [*you act*] thus [*towards Israel*], [*you*] make a woman of me![21] Kill me, I pray thee!' Rashi explains: 'Moses's strength declines like that of a woman (*ki-nekevah*)'. Faced with the prospect of the calamity that God will visit upon his people (his child), Moses breaks down, becomes feeble, collapses like a woman (like a mother). He/she would rather die than see that.

Needless to say, this emergence of the 'feminine' in Moses is not unambiguous. Associated with maternity, it is a moment of weakness. Only when God makes him a mother, and his strength deserts him, does Moses become a woman. This femininity arouses mixed and, at first sight, negative feelings in him: rebellion and a death wish. Unless, of course, we reverse the terms of this observation. Perhaps it is the rebellion itself that makes of Moses a woman: rebellion against the fate God plans for Israel; rebellion against the thankless, untenable role God wants his prophet to play; rebellion against God himself. The articulation of this rebellion and death wish, moreover, is not unavailing.

Certainly, after having given the people the meat they demanded, God severely punishes the rebels, raining death on them, as commemorated in the name given to the site of their rebellion: *Kivrot ha-Ta'avah*, the 'Graves of Craving' (Num 11:33). But God otherwise gives in to Moses: he accepts to release him from part of 'the burden of all this people'. Henceforth, he will be assisted by seventy elders. God thus ratifies Moses's desire not to be everything for Israel; in a way, he ratifies his invocation of weakness and 'takes of the spirit that is upon him, and gives it unto the seventy elders' (Num 11:25). Moses's greatness and primacy are thus preserved, but they now find expression in the acceptance, by God and Moses alike, of a sharing of power and of the burden of responsibility. Joshua, servant of Moses and a warrior at heart, takes fright and tries to intervene: 'My lord Moses, forbid them' (Num 11:28). But Moses will have none of it. He adopts this power-sharing, desires it, would like it to be even broader, extending beyond the narrow circle of the seventy elders: 'Would God that all the Lord's people were prophets, and that the Lord would put his spirit upon them!' (Num 11:29).

Lapsus

There is another point in the Pentateuch where the prophet appears as a feminine 'you'. It is found near the start of Deuteronomy. Moses resumes the narrative of the theophany on Sinai. He recalls how the Hebrews, mightily impressed by this grandiose revelation of the Divine, were also utterly terrified by it. This fright, Moses tells us, was expressed as follows:

> Behold, the Lord our God hath shewed us his glory and his greatness, and we have heard his voice out of the midst of the fire: we have seen this day that God doth talk with man, and he liveth. Now therefore why should we die? for this great fire will consume us: if we hear the voice of the Lord our God any more, then we shall die. For who is there of all flesh, that hath heard the voice of the living God speaking out of the midst of the fire, as we have, and lived? (Deut 5:24–26)

This fear impels the Hebrews to shuffle off onto Moses what is at once an honour, a responsibility, and a higher duty: to hear the Word of the Lord directly, to receive the Law revealed by this Word. This honour, this responsibility, this higher duty are renounced by the Hebrews for themselves and delegated to Moses. Let him take the risk of being consumed by the divine fire![22] 'Go thou [*atah*] near, and hear all that the Lord our God shall say: and speak thou [*at*] unto us all that the Lord our God shall speak unto thee' (Deut 5:27).

Attentive readers will note a strange switch in these statements of Israel as reported by Moses. At the outset, when he says 'Go *thou* near', Moses, who is in the course of reminding Israel of what it said to him on that occasion, puts the verb in the masculine; and the pronoun is likewise in the masculine (*atah*), which is how it should be, given that a man is being referred to. And then, suddenly, when he puts in the people's mouth 'and speak thou [*at*] unto us', while he keeps the verb in the masculine (*tedabber*), the pronoun is in the feminine (*at*, not *atah*). What we have here is not, strictly speaking, what the Hebrews actually said at the time to Moses, but the account Moses gives of it forty years later.[23] On this occasion, then, speaking of himself, the prophet oddly switches from the masculine to the feminine. Might it be that the mere evocation of Israel's refusal to hear the Lord so upsets Moses – he 'of uncircumcised lips' – that he stammers, has trouble expressing himself, replaces one pronoun by another, or does not fully articulate the pronoun (*atah*) and amputates a syllable (*at*) from it, thus inadvertently feminizing it? According to a Talmudic tradition, Moses is prone to this: when 'his strength declines' (under the impact of emotion), he suddenly loses the strength 'to speak', before of course pulling himself together.[24] Just a lapsus, then?

But why shouldn't this lapsus be 'revealing'? Rashi does not hesitate to reveal what he sees as its underlying meaning, adopting a formula with which we are now familiar:

> *You have diminished my strength like that of a woman (ki-nekevah).* I have suffered because of you; you have

enfeebled my hands, for I have seen that you were not eager to approach him out of love. Was it not finer for you to learn from the mouth of the All-Powerful [himself, directly] than to learn through my mediation?

There is definitely something more than a lapsus going on. Not unjustifiably, Moses is once again feminized here. Sheer weakness? Despondency? Sudden – and temporary – exhaustion of the prophet when faced with the ordeal his people, shirking their natural duty, are subjecting him to? I do not think so. On this occasion again, Moses's feminization is the expression of a rebellion – his own rebellion when confronted with his people's want of courage; and the expression of an aspiration – a frustrated one – to sharing. Moses does not want to be so alone; he does not want to be so great. He has only one desire, which is, alas, thwarted: that all his people, like him and with him, should hear and receive the Word of the Lord without fear.

Above and beyond Moses's strength lies therefore a weakness, a frailty. But this weakness and frailty are an even greater strength. In the end, Moses is never greater than when renouncing being Moses; and never more of a man than when he is also a woman. Here as elsewhere, the Pentateuch proves to be something other than the record of Moses's encounter with the Divine – namely, an account of his steep, demanding path towards a fully assumed humanity. Along the way, the embrace of a femininity that is more a desire to share power and responsibility than merely an expression of weakness or fatigue proves to be a necessary step. However, this step is by no means the last. It will be necessary to add to it the embrace of failure and even sin.

5

Divine Snares

'Moses was an hundred and twenty years old when he died' (Deut 34:7). One hundred and twenty – the best age to die. In accordance with a divine decree issued on the eve of the Flood,[1] our ticket is no longer valid beyond that point. Moses was a man, a mere mortal, like us. He therefore had to die one day. But, since he was an exceptional, highly meritorious being, he was allowed to live for as long as a man possibly can on this earth. Viewed thus, Moses's end emerges in a rather comforting light. The longevity is what counts. This eliminates some of the tragedy from the event, rendering his death itself less significant. His life was bound to end and so it did. But it ended late, and ended well.

The wonderful clarity of the prophet's end may be somewhat misleading, however. A snide observer will not fail to remark that, following the promulgation of the famous decree and prior to Moses, quite a few lived a good deal longer. Let us confine ourselves to the Patriarchs: Abraham, 175 (Gen 25:7); Isaac, 180

(Gen 35:28); Jacob, 147 (Gen 47:28). Was Moses lesser in stature than them? It's not that simple, of course. The question suddenly appears rather pointless. The number loses its importance. One hundred and twenty years give or take is perhaps not the real issue. The issue is this death and this particular manner of death, after all. Not all that limpid, in truth. And not all that natural. Is not the account we are given of it slightly disconcerting? It is enough to scratch the surface for this to become blindingly obvious. Tragedy is not so easily eluded.

Moses did not die of old age. Yes, he was 120, but in good health: 'his eye was not dim, nor his natural force abated' (Deut 34:7). Unlike Abraham, he did not die 'in a good old age, old and sated', peacefully 'gathered to his people' (Gn 25: 8). Nor did he die like David, 'old and stricken in years' (I Kgs 1:1). Moses died at the age of 120, but he was not old. Not sated, not happy, not satisfied.

We do not know who buried him. Certainly not his sons, unlike Abraham who was laid to rest by 'Isaac and Ishmael' (Gen 25:9), even though they were *frères ennemis*. We do not even know where he was buried. His tomb has still not been located. Unlike Abraham, who rests beside Sarah his wife in the Cave of Machpelah, bought by him for cash from Ephron the Hittite. Unlike David, buried in the city that bears his name, conquered by him from the Jebusites. Buried only God knows where outside the borders of the Holy Land, nor was Moses entitled to the treatment accorded Joseph, who died in Egypt: no transfer of his ashes to Canaan was ever envisaged, ordered or effected.[2]

Every death, even the putatively natural, is violence done to the living being. Yet the body's deterioration prepares for it, explains it and possibly justifies it: nothing of the sort occurred in Moses's case. The prospect of the homage of descendants and burial in a named, cherished land may soften the blow of death: again, nothing of the kind for Moses. Moses dies alone, in a foreign land, and 'no man knoweth of his sepulchre unto this day' (Deut 34:6). Unnatural, this death seems as violent as a violent death in the literal sense, possibly more so. Moses knows he is going to die; he knows the day and the time; he does not console himself with the illusion of a possible reprieve. And this ineluctable, fixed death is announced by him to Israel: 'I am an hundred and twenty years old this day; I can no more go out and come in' (Deut 31:2). If he 'can no more' come and go, is this because he no longer has the energy? Not at all. If he 'can no more', it is quite simply because God has decided thus. He will go no further, not because his strength has deserted him, but because God has forbidden him. Coming and going, continuing on the path . . . He not only has the energy, but also the desire: 'I pray thee, let me go over' (Deut 3:25), he implores. The request is rejected: 'Let it suffice thee; speak no more unto me of this matter' (Deut 3:26). What God has decided, God will carry out. Or not, for it is not God but Moses who will carry it out. As an ultimate violence, Moses's death is literally a commandment to him from God: 'Die in the mount whither thou goest up' (Deut 32:50). An incredible imperative.

Incredible and cruel. Moses's death is worse than violent; it is cruel. God inflicts more than the pain of death itself on the prophet. He makes him a witness of his own demise. Moses announces it to his people. Furthermore, he himself writes the account of it, just as he had written the remainder of the five books attributed to him:

So Moses the servant of the Lord died there in the land of Moab, according to the word of the Lord. And he was buried

in a valley in the land of Moab, over against Beth-Peor: but
no man knoweth of his sepulchre unto this day. And Moses
was an hundred and twenty years old when he died: his eye
was not dim, nor his natural force abated (Deut 34:5–7).

According to some, admittedly, these verses, like those that
follow (briefly evoking Israel's mourning, his successor Joshua's
'spirit of wisdom', and the incomparable grandeur of the deceased
prophet) – verses with which Deuteronomy and hence the
Pentateuch conclude – were written not by Moses, but by the self-
same Joshua. This seems logical and in accordance with the
limits of a human nature. However, it is far from certain.

For were we not told a little earlier that Moses 'made an end
of writing the words of this law in a book, until they were
finished' (Deut 31:24)? Can the 'book of the law', given by
Moses to the Levites to be placed 'in the side of the ark of the
covenant of the Lord', that it may be there 'for a witness' (Deut
31:26), conceivably be incomplete; might some final verses be
missing, or even a single letter? No. Moses remains the Lord's
prophet 'to the end'. God dictates to him the account of his own
death. And Moses transcribes it faithfully. *Be-dema*, indicates
Rashi: 'while weeping'.[3]

The Prophet's Tears
Why does he weep? Because he is about to die? To suggest as
much is to attribute to Moses an additional, irreducible element
of humanity. What human being does not weep over his or her
own death? Even this prophet, 'whom the Lord knew face to
face' and whose 'like' has not been seen 'since in Israel' (Deut
34:10), is said to have wept over his own death. Because he is
also a human being, a plain human being. Unless, of course, it is

not the man, but instead the prophet who sheds tears on this occasion. The man might well weep before the prospect of death. The prophet weeps at not having finished his mission; he weeps out of a sense of incompletion. Moses has freed the Hebrews from slavery in Egypt; he has communicated the Law to them; for forty years he has guided them through the desert. Yet it is not he, but Joshua, who will lead them into the Land promised to their ancestors. Moses will have seen with his own eyes only the start of the fulfilment of the Promise: 'thou has begun to shew thy servant thy greatness, and thy mighty hand', he says to the Lord (Deut 3:24). But God will not allow him to witness its conclusion: 'thou shalt not go over this Jordan' (Deut 3:27). At most he will offer him a tiny compensation. From on high and from afar, from the summit of the mountain where he is going to die, he will be able to see that Land he will never tread.

Rashi, interpreting the few verses in Deuteronomy 34 on this overview of the Holy Land from afar, granted the prophet *in extremis*, would go much further. It is not only 'all the land of Gilead, unto Dan, And all Naphtali, and the land of Ephraim, and Manasseh, and all the land of Judah, unto the utmost sea, And the south, and the plain of the valley of Jericho, the city of the palm trees, unto Zoar' (Deut 34:1-3), that is shown by God to the prophet and which the prophet sees. For Moses is a prophet, a seer, and what he sees, and what God reveals to him, is not only a territory, a space, geography. It is time – history – that he sees and which God reveals to him: the whole future history of Israel in this territory – the long, tumultuous history of its prosperity, destruction and renaissance – and, far beyond the bounds of this territory, the history of the whole world, from its creation to the resurrection of the dead, to the last days. Does not a Midrash suggest reading, in place of 'unto the utmost sea (*yam*)', 'unto the utmost day (*yom*)'?[4]

In a way, if we follow the commentator, this final, total revelation confirms Moses in his status of absolute, insuperable prophet. He is even graced with a form of immortality in the present moment. By the same token, he is nonetheless brought back down to the insurmountable limits of his own mortality, since (Rashi tells us) if God has shown him all that – the land 'which I sware unto Abraham, unto Isaac, and unto Jacob' (Deut 34:4), and the history of the land and of the people that is going to inherit it – it is precisely because Moses will not experience it: 'I have caused thee to see it with thine eyes, but thou shalt not go over thither' (Deut 34:4). Moses will not experience the fulfilment of the Promise: he is only the distant, passive, prophetic spectator of it. And God makes him its spectator only so that in the place where he is going – the kingdom of the dead – he can tell the Patriarchs that the promise made them has been (and will be) kept: 'In order that you go and say to Abraham, Isaac and Jacob: the Holy One, blessed be his name, has fulfilled the pledge he made to you.'[5]

Moses is absolutely a prophet, on at least two levels: he has seen (fore-seen) the whole history of the world; and he has, without omitting a single letter, transcribed the whole Torah revealed to him by God, including the account of his own death. If he weeps while writing the narrative of that death at God's dictation, it is perhaps simply because it betokens the incompletion of his vocation on a third level: that of action. Condemned to be no more than a spectator of the realization of the Promise (the Hebrews taking possession of their Land), he ceases to be what he has been until now: an agent of this process. This incompletion forever marks the destiny of the greatest of prophets. There will always be something that Moses was unable to do, that God would not let him do. As if God himself, forcing him to die at this point – before the crossing of the Jordan – and not a little later, just a fraction later, was condemning Moses to abandon the mission he had entrusted him with. God has indeed achieved his own design: to prevent Moses from (fully) accomplishing his mission.

From the outset, Moses was threatened with death. At the time of his birth, by Pharaoh's murderous decree directed at the first-born males of Israel. At the moment of his abandonment, by the waters of the Nile that might well engulf him. When he kills one of the Egyptians persecuting Israel, he must flee another death sentence, seeking refuge in the land of Midian. Death once again stalks him on the night of his return to Egypt, and Zipporah will save him from it. And it is again death that lies in wait when God reveals himself to him, 'for . . . no man [shall] see me, and live' (Exod 33:20). However – and this emerges clearly at the time of Moses's actual death – the threat that Moses's possible death has suspended over him at every turn was not so much of his demise as of the interruption of his mission. Time after time, the very God who has entrusted Moses with this mission threatens to render its accomplishment impossible. God, who is always having second thoughts. Because God is like that. And because man (Moses is a man) is like that: condemned to incompletion. And, at the end, when the end really does come, God wins and man loses, and hence Moses too loses: he will not see, cannot see, his mission through to the end. In these circumstances, no wonder he writes the account of his own death *be-dema*, 'in tears'. It is not his death that makes him cry, but what it means.

However, Moses has fought well. He has stood his ground. One hundred and twenty years: not bad at all, in the end, especially when you bear such a burden – an entire people to free and a whole Law to teach – and you have with you, but also facing you, not to say against you, such a Partner. In fact, Moses might well never have died, had he not sinned. And he might well never have sinned. So, God took precautions. God fixed it, so as to be sure of achieving his ends. He made Moses sin. He set a trap for him. And Moses fell right into it. Because he was a man, after all, and had forgotten that God is not always loyal.

A trap? More like two, in fact.

Here is the first.

The Episode of the Explorers

At the start of the Book of Deuteronomy, Moses mentions an unhappy episode – the so-called episode of the explorers – which is, at least indirectly and as if by contamination, the reason for his condemnation, if not to die, then at least not to set foot in the Promised Land.

This episode is narrated for the first time in Chapter 13 of the Book of Numbers. It seems to open with the expression of a divine wish: 'Send thou men, that they may search the land of Canaan' (Num 13:2). Moses obeys. Twelve men, one per tribe, are dispatched to find out what the land the Hebrews must take possession of, and the people settled on it, are like. The twelve soon return and report back. Yes, the land they have visited 'floweth with milk and honey' and yields wonderful fruits (Num 13:27). One problem: the people who live there are large, powerful, and probably invincible. Ten of the twelve scouts manage to dissuade Israel from joining battle. Only Caleb and Joshua, Moses's future successor, exhort the Hebrews not to give up, to remember that the Lord is with them, and to prepare for conquest. In a fit of rage, God initially envisages sending a plague to wipe out the whole community of rebels and defeatists, and begetting from Moses himself 'a greater nation and mightier than they' (Num 13:12).[6] As might be expected, the prophet rejects such an outcome and pleads for mercy. With relative success, as usual. Israel will not be destroyed. On the other hand, all adults over the age of twenty – with the exception of Caleb and Joshua – will die in the desert, in the course of forty years of wandering. Only Caleb, Joshua and the descendants of this 'evil congregation' (Num 14:27) will have the right, at the end of this terrible cleansing, to cross the Jordan and enter the Holy Land. Here nothing is said of Moses. He is obviously one of the over-twenties and belongs to the generation that experienced Egypt and slavery. His name is not cited among those who might escape the verdict. He is not explicitly condemned, but nor is he expressly absolved, even though God briefly considered making him the father of a new people destined to replace Israel. Here we have an initial ambiguity that does not bode well.

As a matter of fact, at the start of Deuteronomy, recalling this unhappy episode this time in the first person, Moses himself dispels the ambiguity: 'Also with me the Lord was angry because of you, saying, Thou also shalt not go in thither. But Joshua the son of Nun, which standeth before thee, he shall go in thither' (Deut 1:37). Moses will not, then, escape the fate allotted to the desert generation: '*Thou also* (*gam-ata*) shalt not go in thither', the Lord says to him. Like all the rest, he will die without being able to cross the Jordan. However, two words attract our attention in these statements by Moses: '*Also with me* (*gam-bi*) the Lord was angry *because of you* (*biglalkhem*)'. And the ambiguity we thought had been cleared up suddenly re-emerges in a different guise. It is a curious formula that simultaneously associates Moses with the community of rebels ('me also') and distinguishes him from it ('because of you'). As if Moses were sharing the punishment without having shared the transgression; as if he were being punished along with others for the sin of others. This does not make a Christ of him; he does not pay for all the others. But it makes him pay for a sin committed by others, not by him.

Moses's account of the episode at the start of Deuteronomy, rather different from that in Numbers, clarifies the likely reasons for the ambiguity. The idea of sending explorers into Canaan came neither from God nor from Moses. The request was made to Moses by the Hebrews themselves: 'And ye came near unto me every one of you, and said, We will send men before us . . .' (Deut 1:22). Here, clearly distinguished, we have Moses on one side and the whole community of Israel on the other. Moses pursues his narrative thus: 'the saying pleased me' (Deut 1:23). The prophet agrees with the communal view and ratifies it. In so doing, he becomes part of this community; he is not opposed to it and he is not distinguished from it. The popular will has been expressed, it is unanimous ('every one of you'), and Moses gives effect to it. In this context, there is of course an absence to be noted: God does not feature in the exchange. As if the theocratic principle had yielded to a democratic principle. As if Moses were no longer the designated mediator in a superior dialogue, that between God and his people, with the former commanding from above and the latter obeying below. This time the request comes from below. In this matter, Moses consults only the people. And since the latter are unanimous, as Abraham Ibn Ezra stresses, Moses, who has become a simple 'representative of the people', acquiesces and acts.

A question naturally arises here. The sanction applies to Moses and the desert generation: that much is clear. The reason for the sanction against the desert generation is also clear: for having refused to set about conquering the Land promised to it and, by the same token, having lacked trust in God. This is exactly what Moses says to the Hebrews: 'In this thing ye did not believe the Lord your God' (Deut 1:32). It is just as clear that 'this thing' cannot be held against Moses himself. On the contrary, he did not fail to enjoin courage and confidence: 'Dread not, neither be afraid of them. The Lord your God which goeth before you, he shall fight for you' (Deut 1:29-30). While the penalty is the same for Moses and the desert generation, its motivation cannot be identical. So, could it be that what is held against Moses is that he played the 'democrat', adhering without further ado to the decision democratically and, what's more, unanimously taken by the people to send explorers into Canaan? That, when the people came to him with its proposal, he waived requesting divine assent and thus flatly abdicated his prophetic status? Is Moses guilty of democratic humility?

This interpretation is undeniably appealing. However, it is rather too flattering to our secular reflexes. Moses as the first separator of Church and State? What the people (Israel) wants, the State (Moses) effects, without reference to any Church (God). This is all very nice – a little too nice. Whether we like it or not, God is part and parcel of the narrative. Similarly, we cannot strip Moses of his prophet's garb just like that. God is there, and at no point does Moses cease to be his prophet. He knows that the people's initiative is displeasing to God. When he states 'the saying pleased me', he implies: 'but not God'.[7] Rashi explains: 'I [Moses] agreed with you, hoping that you would review your decision when you saw that I was not opposed to it, but you did not change your mind'. Moses's fault might therefore be that he tempted the people: that he remained silent (did not explicitly inform them of divine reservations), in order to see if Israel would of its own accord withdraw its proposal, and in the hope (it seems) that it would do so. Moses's fault may well have been that he (prematurely) tested the democratic and theological maturity of a people that had only just emerged from slavery. As if, without their prophet guiding them, at least indirectly, without his inviting God to intervene at all in the debate, the people were already somehow capable on their own of understanding that to launch such an exploration was, in and of itself, evidence of a lack of trust in God and obviously could not please him. Was Moses the tempter of his people, deliberately not warning them of the trap they were laying for themselves? Is it for this that God later sanctions Moses? Is this how we should understand 'Also with me the Lord was angry because of you' (Deut 1:37)? Is Moses guilty of having deliberately made his people fall into the trap of the democratic temptation?

This second interpretation is no less appealing than the first. It differs from it only by the extra dramatic tension it introduces into the story, Moses toying with his people and God allowing him to do it. Obviously, this dimension cannot be excluded. God only steps in after the event, only when all the sins have been irremediably committed, only when the time has come just to punish. The people stray. Moses lets the people stray. And God lets Moses act that way. Who is really toying with whom? Who is tempting whom here?

To be certain, the best thing is to return to the original account of the episode of the explorers (that in Numbers), and to its first two verses: 'And the Lord spake unto Moses, saying, Send thou men, that they may search the land of Canaan, which I give unto the children of Israel' (Num 13:1–2). Everything looks straightforward here. The initiative would not appear to proceed from either the people or Moses. As so often, God communicates an apparently clear order to Moses. And, as always, Moses carries out the divine order: 'And Moses by the commandment of the Lord sent them' (Num 13:3). Everything seems to be in order. And if the people eventually draw faulty conclusions from their exploration (we must not go there!), and are punished for that, we may well wonder what sin Moses has committed to warrant his being sanctioned as well.

If various rabbinical sources are to be believed, however, the opening of Chapter 13 of Numbers should be regarded as elliptical. The idea of sending scouts into the Holy Land definitely came from the community of Israel, which submitted it to Moses (as reported in Deuteronomy). What these sources add is that Moses did consult the Lord. And this is how the latter responded: 'I have told them that [the land] is good . . . For the life of them! I shall lead them astray, following the report of the explorers, so that they shall not inherit it!'[8] The people's initiative is not pleasing to God: it betrays a lack of trust in his word. Consequently, God decides to encourage it solely in order to give them the opportunity to go all the way in their offence – and to give himself the opportunity to punish them in the most terrible way, by depriving them for a generation of possession of this 'land flowing with milk and honey' (Exod 3:17). Israel has trapped itself in a process that God chooses not to halt. The people have sinned already and God lures them on, literally setting a trap so that they sin further and are further punished.

But is this God who sets a trap for Israel not, by the same token, ensnaring Moses himself? In telling him: 'Send *thou* men, that they may search the land of Canaan', he only pretends to give him an order. God does not say to him: 'Send men', but 'Send *thou* men' (*shelah lekha*). This means: on your own initiative, since it is your idea, very well, send these scouts into Canaan . . . Has Moses understood? Has he paid attention to every single word spoken to him by God and has he spotted the implication? Does he perceive that this order is not an order, that it only conveys the impression of being one, that it is a mere concession by God? And that if, a little later, it is said of him (Moses) that he acts '[according to the word] of the Lord' (Num 13:3), this means nothing other than 'with his permission', 'without his preventing him'?[9] Just when Moses may think he is obeying a divine command, he is really contravening it. God sets a trap for his prophet and his prophet falls into it. An inadvertent sinner, a sinner despite himself, well might Moses say that 'the Lord was angry with me because of you' (Deut 1:37). He might equally have said, because of him.

End of the tale of the first trap.

The Water of Meribah

God has the right and the power to cause his prophet to stumble. His intention – and who would dare hold it against him? – is simply to ensure that Moses never exceeds the limits of the human condition. Moses is a man and must remain one, which means: sinner, mortal, condemned to incompletion. This confirmation of Moses' frailty cannot, however, occur at the cost of the sheer abolition of his greatness. The prophet must remain immense so that the incomparable value of his prophecy is preserved.

Now, Moses's greatness seems to be guaranteed by the very disproportion between the offence he is accused of and the penalty inflicted on him. The offence, which seems slight indeed, is almost cancelled out by the existence of the trap that induces it. The sin being inadvertent, it certainly does not amount to much, at least in the absolute. By contrast, the punishment is very severe. However, we should not be surprised. On the contrary. For the penalty is calculated to be commensurate, not with the gravity of the sin committed, but with the stature of he who committed it. Had it been someone other than Moses, he would certainly have paid less dearly. 'The Holy One, blessed be his name, proves fastidious with the Righteous'[10] – even when they only deviate from the right path by 'a hair's breadth'.[11] The greatest of all need hardly do a thing to incur the most dreadful punishment. Paradoxically, the tenuousness of his sin and the severity of the penalty attest to the greatness of the man Moses and confirm it.

However, it is not enough to preserve that greatness. It is not enough that Moses is a great man. It is further necessary that he should be an exceptional Hebrew. The tale of the explorers foments a possible confusion. The heights of exegetical subtlety were required to show that, while the sanction is the same for Moses and the desert generation, the _cause_ of the sanction is not exactly the same for both. The desert generation is punished for not having trusted its God; Moses, for having rashly, perhaps inadvertently, conceded its request. Even so, the two sins – Israel's major one and Moses's minor one – are closely linked, the prophet and his people seeming to be encompassed in the same censure and ultimately affected by the same sanction.

The biblical tradition, along with the rabbinical tradition that follows, adopts and inflects it, are manifestly loath to run such a risk. To guarantee the greatness of Moses the Hebrew, the ideal thing would be to hit upon a fault that _he alone_ committed, which could in no way be confused with any offence by Israel. The ideal would be to find for him, and for his brother Aaron who is likewise destined to die in the desert, an offence that distinguishes them from the common herd of Israel. To be great, one must stand out from the little people by one's sin as well as virtues. This distinctive sin, the sin that paradoxically magnifies, will be found in another incident known as the Water of Meribah, or the 'Waters of Quarrelling' (Num 20:13). 'Had it not been for this sin', Rashi tells us, 'they would have entered into the Land [of Israel]'.[12] Thanks to it, he adds, 'no one will be able to say that they were punished for the same fault as the desert generation.'

What is this about? One of the numerous occasions when Israel complains. Not of hunger but of thirst, as it happens. And not for the first time. However, the moment is significant. Forty years have passed. The desert generation has perished, with the exception of Moses and Aaron (I omit Caleb and Joshua, who are to be spared). Miriam, their sister, has herself just died. Yet the community – of the generation that grew up in the desert, since they are the only ones left – is suddenly short of water and picks a quarrel with Moses and his brother. The scenario is a classic one.

What happens in Chapter 20 of the Book of Numbers (verses 1–13) contains echoes of what occurred forty years earlier, in Exodus 17 (verses 1–7). It was not the same people then, but the parents of the present generation. Unlike today, they were not on the eve of their entry into the Holy Land, but on the morrow of their crossing of the Red Sea. The people were thirsty and picked a quarrel with Moses, who turned to God. He ordered his prophet to go ahead of the people, take some of the elders with him, and to arm himself with the staff with which he had already performed various miracles; and he said to him: 'Behold, I will stand before thee there upon the rock in Horeb; and thou shalt smite the rock, and there shall come water out of it, that the people may drink' (Exod 17:6). Which is what Moses did, rigorously, and the water flowed.

Four decades later, with the descendants of the first generation of rebels, Moses and Aaron (since they are now associates) might have a feeling of déjà vu. God appears to them and says: 'Take the staff, and gather thou the assembly together, thou, and Aaron thy brother, and speak ye unto the rock before their eyes; and it shall give forth his water, and thou shalt bring forth to them water out of the rock: so thou shalt give the congregation and their beasts drink' (Num 20:8). Moses and Aron assemble the community before the rock, Moses raises his hand, strikes the rock with his staff 'twice' (Num 20:11), and water flows from it in abundance.

The parallelism of the two accounts is clearly misleading. Their conclusions are entirely antithetical. Whereas, forty years earlier, Israel was condemned for having picked a quarrel with Moses and for having 'tempted' the Lord, saying: 'Is the Lord among us, or not?' (Exod 17:7), this time it is Moses and Aron who are in the frame: 'Because ye believed me not, to sanctify me in the eyes of the children of Israel, therefore ye shall not bring this congregation in to the land which I have given them' (Num 20:12). If there has been an offence, this time it was committed by the prophet and his brother. But what exactly is the offence?

The repetition is an illusion. This time, God did not ask Moses (and Aaron) to strike the rock, but to speak to it: 'speak ye unto the rock' (Num 20:8). Moses took up his staff, as commanded by God. But then he thought he should simply repeat the gesture of yesteryear: he said nothing to the rock, but struck it, as he had done forty years before, and (what's more) struck it twice. A miracle occurred, but not the one desired by God. Whereas the Exodus generation was rewarded by an ordinary miracle – a rock which, when struck by the prodigious staff, split to supply it with water to drink – the generation of the entry into the Holy Land may well have needed a different miracle: less material, more spiritual, not derived from the brutal, coarse contact of wood and stone, but simply from the prophet's words, which would have been 'heard', as it were, by the rock. As Rashi points out, the lesson the Hebrews would have drawn from this, by which God would genuinely have been 'sanctified' among them, would have been very different. 'They would have said: "If the rock, which does not speak or hear, and has no need of food, accomplishes the word of God, how much more [must we obey it]!"' So, did Moses, the prophet of the old generation – of slavery, Exodus, the Revelation and the desert – here betray his incapacity to become the prophet of the new generation – of freedom in the Law and conquest of the Land? To such an extent that there now remains for him, as for his brother, only one way of 'sanctifying' the Lord 'in the eyes of the children of Israel', in other words, to the new generation: by dying, punished for the offence they have committed, thus showing ordinary mortals that even God's saints do not escape his righteous judgement?[13]

Through their sin, Moses and Aaron might still seem to be somewhat bound up with the desert generation. But it does not mark them out any the less: it is their own sin, they have committed it, and it is because – almost by virtue – of this singular sin that they will be forbidden to cross the Jordan. What is more, in and through the punishment inflicted on them for this singular sin, they become – despite themselves – the tools of a lesson imparted to the new generation. For those who survive them, the death that strikes them remains a life lesson. The boundary they come up against is one more opening.

A Rock that Disappears

But can we leave it at that? The account of the Meribah incident is in fact far murkier than the water springing from its rock. It is one of those elliptical, confused passages in which the Bible abounds. One question certainly remains hanging: how could Moses, who was hardly venturing on his first exchange with Heaven, strike the rock when God had told him to speak to it? This crucial question cannot be resolved before we have clarified, if possible, the precise sequence of events.

Let us begin, then, with the essential thing: the rock. I say *the* rock. What does the definite article signify? It is rather as if God was pointing out to Moses and Aaron a very specific rock, distinct from all the rest, in a desert that is not short of them. 'Speak ye unto *the* rock', he tells them (Num 20:8). Likewise, it is before *the* rock that they assemble the thirsty community (Num 20:10). Next, curiously, they question the capacity of '*this* rock' to supply water to the people (Num 20:10). And finally, Moses strikes '*the* rock' twice. Are we necessarily always dealing with the same rock? The one God points to as a possible source; the one Moses and Aaron doubt can perform this role; and the one, ultimately, that provides water to the thirsty – are these one and the same rock? Finally, when Moses strikes '*the* rock', why does he strike it twice? Wouldn't once have been enough?

What is betrayed by the confusion of a narration that might be called strangely 'garbled', as if Moses, the 'stammering' prophet, proved here as self-conscious when it comes to writing as he is at speaking? Is the uncertainty of the account anything other than the expression or continuation of that which seems to have seized its protagonists when they experienced what is recounted? In which case a question remained mysterious to them, almost to the end: the rock? But which rock?

A Midrashic tradition, partially adopted and summarized by Rashi, offers an answer. To start with, it observes that the lack of water affects the people as soon as Miriam, sister of Moses and Aaron, dies. We know that, thanks to Miriam's merit, a 'well' accompanied the Hebrews throughout their forty years' trek through the desert.[14] The day of her death, this 'well' dries up and thirst descends. The 'well' or 'spring' enjoyed by the Hebrews in the desert was none other than the one Moses had caused to gush from the rock he had struck forty years before, on the morrow of the Exodus, when the people were thirsty for the first time. The rock of which God speaks to Moses and Aaron is precisely that one: the rock that provided them with water four decades earlier, which, thanks to their sister's merit, has accompanied them all this time and just dried up on her death. Doubtless this can only encourage the return of an old reflex: must this rock, which once was struck, really now be spoken to?

That said, suddenly the rock cannot be located: Moses and Aaron can no longer identify it. Once the spring has dried up, the miraculous rock has become one rock among others. It has left, gone missing, got lost, become indiscernible among the rocks that fill the landscape. Moses and Aaron search for the missing rock, but in vain. The people challenge them, perhaps suspect them of playing for time, employing cunning, or using their experience as desert shepherds, perfectly capable of finding water (without resort to miracles) where no one would suspect it of being concealed: 'What does it matter what rock you extract water from?'[15] This is the question Moses and Aaron respond to, saying: 'Hear now, ye rebels [*i.e. rebels against us, Moses and Aaron, your masters*]; must we fetch you water out of this rock [*this nondescript rock, which you point out to us at random and for which we have received no command from God*]?' (Num 20:10).

Moses and Aaron, prostrated with grief for their sister and harassed by an aggressive crowd, lose patience, become annoyed, and deal with the most pressing problem. Perhaps they speak to the rock indicated by the people at random and nothing issues from it. They remember their past experience and think: 'Maybe we need to strike it, like the first time'. Moses strikes the rock – the nondescript one, or perhaps the one God has finally enabled them to identify – once. And a few drops come out.[16] Then Moses strikes it a second time and the water flows abundantly.

Is that how it happened? Or differently? It does not really matter. Mourning, fatigue, anger, the temptation to simply repeat a gesture whose efficacy has already been demonstrated – all of this conspires to distract Moses from a strict, rigorous observance of God's instructions. How should things have unfolded had everything proceeded normally, in complete accordance with God's intention? Differently, no doubt. But it remains difficult to spell out. There is something like a diabolical mechanism at work here. This rock, first of all, which dries up, absconds and disappears, becoming indiscernible, only to reappear when it is too late – when Moses, doubtful, hesitant, caught between the impatience of a febrile people and the clarity, already slightly blurred, of the divine command, has lost the thread of righteous conduct. The rock that finally he strikes just to have done with it, instead of speaking to it. Did I say a diabolical mechanism? No, rather a divine snare. It would not be the first. As if God had at once created and exploited a situation where, prisoners of an inexorable process, Moses and Aaron could finally do nothing but sin. It is easy for God to then say: 'Because *ye believed me not* (*lo-he'emantem bi*), to sanctify me in the eyes of the children of Israel, therefore ye shall not bring this congregation into the land which I have given them' (Num

20:12). Divine bad faith and cruel irony! Forty years earlier, it was Moses who berated the desert generation and its explorers: 'in this thing ye did not believe [*einkhem ma'aminim*] the Lord your God' (Deut 1:32). Today, forty years later, it is Moses and Aaron whom God has the cheek to rebuke for a similar failing, doing so in identical terms!

A Spring that Dries Up

Moses and Aaron. Moses is no longer on his own. This time, the two of them fall into the trap of sin laid by God. In fact, there are three of them united in a common destiny, for it is the death of Miriam, their sister, that unleashes the episode fatal to both men. Soon Moses too will die, this side of the Jordan, 'at the commandment of the Lord' or 'by the mouth of the Lord' (*al-pi ha-shem*) (Deut 34:5). But before him it is Aaron, his elder by three years (according to Exodus 7:7), who will die, likewise 'at the commandment of the Lord' or 'by the mouth of the Lord'. Miriam herself, Tradition informs us, perished 'by the mouth of the Lord' – in a divine kiss – and if the Torah does not expressly mention this, it is out of modesty and respect for the divine Presence.[17]

Moses is no longer alone. He is once more his brother's brother and his sister's brother. But this time in death. Aaron, his spokesman, leaves him, abandoning him to his poor stammering voice as a prophet with a wounded body. Miriam, who had saved him, watching over him as an infant adrift in a basket, likewise abandons him to a now certain death. Buried there (*sham*), Miriam goes first (Num 20:1). Passing away there (*sham*), Aaron goes next (Num 21:28). And soon Moses in his turn will die there (*sham*) (Deut 34:5). The children of Jochebed and Amram are reunited once more, virtually equal in death. What they chiefly share is to have expired there, *sham*: this side of the Jordan. Sinners each in their own fashion, they are condemned to a single penalty that no longer differentiates between them, and scarcely distinguishes them, either, from the rebel generation that likewise perished in the desert sands. Their sole privilege, if they must have one, is the divine kiss in which they expire.

Moses's death certainly remains exceptional, in more ways than one. But this does not prevent it from being an ordinary death as well. The death of the greatest of prophets, but also the death of a humble sinner. The death of one who has seen, foreseen, the entire history of his people and the entire history of humanity, down to the last day, but also the death of a man who has failed to complete the mission entrusted to him. The death of a man who cannot but die, like every human being, before the age he had dreamed of reaching. Who dies like the rest of us, prematurely.

Moses finally died as he had to die, almost as he was born and almost as he lived: by water. He did not succumb to the waters of the Nile, for his sister, Miriam, watched over him there. He managed to save all his people in the parted waters of the Red Sea and to drown their pursuers in it and Miriam, 'the prophetess, the sister of Aaron', after him and like him, had sung the canticle celebrating victory with all the women (Exod 15:1–21). At the end, it is the water of the rock that undoes him, that seals his loss, the water of the dried-up rock that gushes forth again. The water of the rock of Miriam, her once again. The invariable power of water – and women – over Moses's destiny.

But was this rock simply a rock? Was the water that sprang from it merely water? Others have latched onto the metaphor, to employ it in the way we know. 'They [the Hebrews] drank of that spiritual Rock that followed them: and that Rock was

Christ' (I Cor 10:4). Gregory of Nyssa elaborates: this rock – Christ – 'is inaccessible and resistant to unbelievers, but if one should employ the staff of faith he becomes drink to those who are thirsty and flows into those who receive him'.[18] We don't have to leave this metaphor to Paul, Gregory and co. Is not God himself 'our Rock' (Deut 32:31)? And is not his Torah commonly compared to water? *'Ein mayim ela Torah'*, the Sages teach us. *'Water is only ever invoked to speak of Torah*, as is thus said: "every one that thirsteth, come ye to the waters"' (Isa 55:1).[19]

If this is so, however, if this rock is more than a rock and this water more than water, Israel's sudden thirst on the eve of its entry into the Holy Land must be something more than ordinary thirst. And Moses's sudden difficulty in slaking his people is then more than the result of a fleeting distraction. When striking the rock because he can no longer bring forth from it thirst-quenching water, Moses may be already dead. Just as the water struggles to flow from the stone, Moses is already struggling to elicit the Torah from the divine Rock. He can no longer speak. He can only strike. And if he strikes, it is because he has not clearly understood what God requires of him (to speak to the rock, not strike it). When Moses strikes the rock to extract water from it, it is almost as if he were striking God himself in order to extract a few more drops of Torah. Perhaps it is not the rock that has dried up but Moses himself, with his death on this side of the Jordan confirming a spiritual exhaustion which the vigour of his body and the brightness of his eye cannot completely mask. Moses was the prophet of liberation and revelation. He cannot be the prophet of the Law in action and the conquered Land.

Perhaps this is also what he meant when he said, on his 120th birthday, 'I can no more go out and come in' (Deut 31:2). As we have seen, we should construe this as: 'I am no longer permitted to do so'. But it might also be telling us (as Rashi points out) that he is henceforth unable to 'go and come in the things of the Torah', because 'the traditions and sources of wisdom have been closed to him'.[20] When Aaron is about to die, he bequeaths the priesthood to his descendants: Moses strips him of his garments and clothes his son Eleazar in them (Num 20:28). When Moses himself dies, it is not to one of his sons, but to Joshua, that he hands over leadership of the people. And it is to Israel as a whole that he leaves his only bequest: the Torah. Yet just as he bequeaths it, it escapes him.

In this respect, Moses is a true teacher. To teach is to accept losing.

6

Light and Shadow

Moses after Moses: the story from Moses to the present – what is there to say? Perhaps simply this, which we find at the very beginning of a frequently cited text from old rabbinical literature: 'Moses received (the) Torah from Sinai, and transmitted it to Joshua, and Joshua transmitted it to the Elders, and the Elders to the Prophets, and the Prophets to the members of the Great Assembly.'[1]

Here we have the whole history of Moses down to the present: the history of a reception – by Moses – and then of a transmission, from one generation to the next, of what Moses received. A curious history, very different from the one we have been accustomed to read in the Bible: a history without events, twists and turns, or betrayals; a history without any breaks. In fact, not a history at all. Merely the recall of a founding principle: the seamless continuity of a transmission extending from Moses to the present. The members of the Great Assembly[2] were not, of course, the last staging-posts in this transmission. The chain, solid and secure, has gone on lengthening with each generation, down to our own.

Transmission

The title of the Mishnah* tractate of which the above quotation is the opening passage is ambiguous: *Avot*. It can be understood in two senses: 'Principles' or 'Fathers'. Hence the tractate may be read in two ways: either as a tractate of essentially moral principles, taught by the original masters of the Jewish oral tradition; or as a tractate on the fathers or masters of this tradition, since its first four chapters attribute each reported piece of teaching to a named master, and the first two at least present these teachings in clearly chronological order, thus delineating a veritable genealogy of rabbinical knowledge.

Moses is the first in the chain. This is not insignificant. He is the first to receive and the first to transmit. He is therefore at once a master, the first of masters and the greatest, which comes as no surprise; and a father, which is less commonplace. A father, or the ancestor of a lineage, defined in terms of the spirit and not the flesh, certainly, but a line all the same. Here, Moses figures as an absolute beginning. No one possesses greater salience, or even the advantage of preceding him. The Patriarchs have disappeared; Abraham, Isaac and Jacob are not in the running. The Father and Master is Moses, no one else. And, as if to ground the authority of his prophet, God himself is somehow bracketed. Moses does not receive 'the Torah from God on Sinai', he receives 'the Torah from Sinai'. The formula is unusual, but also welcome. Not only because it speaks to those of us who are secular and from a generation that is perfectly delighted to forego any mention of God, but for another reason: there is nothing and no one here – not even God – to put the prophet in the shade.

A further curiosity of these opening words from the tractate of Fathers is that it does not state that 'Moses received *the* Torah', but simply: 'Moses received *torah*'. No definite article. The concept is broader as a result. It is not simply a matter of *the* Torah in the strict, narrow sense – the five books of Moses, the Pentateuch, the written Law – but of 'Torah' in a more inclusive sense: written Torah and oral Torah combined. It is this Torah, in both its dimensions, that Moses received and transmitted to Israel. Or possibly the oral Torah above all, or exclusively. After all, the written Torah, once written, is transmitted mechanically, materially, objectively: it simply requires custodians of the text, ink, parchment and diligent copyists. The oral Torah follows a different route. It is transmitted from mouth to ear: from God's mouth to Moses's ear, from Moses's mouth to Joshua's ear, and so on indefinitely, from teacher to disciple, from generation to generation down to our own, in a chain that might seem fragile, but whose continuity and reliability the tractate of the Fathers is intent on affirming, from Moses onwards.

This doctrine of dual inheritance is the cornerstone of rabbinical Judaism: no written Law (the letter) without oral Law (the spirit). The meaning of the first remains impenetrable to those unenlightened by insights from the second. And the second is the peculiar, inalienable asset of the people of Israel, the orality and hence relative confidentiality of its transmission preventing impure hands from getting hold of it inappropriately. The permanence of this particular asset, not being guaranteed by the objective materiality of a written support, depends subjectively, directly and exclusively on Israel itself – on the existence within it of the unbroken chain of masters and pupils whose initial links are inventoried by the tractate of Fathers. Moses understood this clearly and, according to an old rabbinical account,[3] found it worrying. Indeed, the prophet supposedly suggested to God (for more security?) transcribing the oral Law! But God, farsighted, was opposed, lest it suffer the same fate as would befall the Bible. The latter's transcription and subsequent translation into Greek ended up making it accessible to everyone, particularly Christians, who would hardly put it to best use. To entrust the oral Law to an exclusively oral transmission was perhaps to imperil it, but at the same time shielded it from alien appropriation.

The initial receiver of both written and oral Law, Moses thus emerges as the absolute receiver of a total knowledge. For us twenty-first-century historicists, the oral Law can only be the gradual development, via successive, datable accretions, of a tradition of teaching enriching itself with the contributions of generations of scholars, who have succeeded one another over the centuries in the most diverse socio-historical contexts. By contrast, rabbinical Judaism persists in inverting the 'natural' logic of things and locating in Moses, and the revelation on Sinai, both the beginning and the end of this tradition. Everything was already there, imparted lock, stock and barrel to the greatest prophet Israel has ever known. After Moses, teaching only makes known the already-revealed, only imparts the already-known. The teacher preserves; he no longer invents.

There is every sign here of Moses possessing absolute, unparalleled greatness. But this absolute greatness at the same time appears somewhat futile. Moses received everything and transmitted everything. But once dead, despite his absolute greatness, he can no longer do anything for the Torah that he received and transmitted. After him, everything depends on the necessarily fragile chain of subsequent receivers and transmitters: Joshua, Elders,

Prophets, members of the Great Assembly, teachers and disciples of all generations down to our own. One weak link, and the chain could break. Once again everything depends on everyone.

And by 'everyone', I today mean female as well as male. This is not some provocation or concession to 'theological correctness'. Jewish women, whether belonging to secular, liberal or even orthodox wings of Judaism, have long emancipated themselves from the limits imposed on their sex for centuries by an exclusively male rabbinical establishment, and have begun to play a full role in transmitting a legacy they have appropriated and enhanced. This cannot even be regarded as a recent novelty. It is a fact, duly rooted in the variegated landscape of contemporary Judaism.

The written Torah still has to be read at each generation. The oral Torah still has to be taught at each generation. There is nothing more fragile than Moses's bequest to his people, and its perpetuation has long ceased to depend on Moses and depends precisely on that people. The imposing Torah of the imposing Moses is at the mercy of the humblest of Israel's children.

'Touch not my messiahs,[4] and do my prophets no harm' (I Chr 16:22). Who is being referred to? According to some,[5] the Lord's (new) 'prophets' are the 'disciples of the Sages' – those whom we would simply call scholars or teachers. And his (new) 'messiahs' are none other than the 'children of the schools'. The heritage is henceforth in their hands. And the very fate of this world, which 'subsists solely by grace of the breath of the children of the schools', hangs on their lips. The greatest of the prophets – Moses – is merely the first of the teachers. And the instruction of the first of teachers is now entirely dependent for its survival on the chain of masters and disciples that follows him – a chain as weak and as necessary as the breathing of a child.

Face-to-Face

That the light brought into this world by Moses must now, to remain visible, be reflected in humbler mirrors, does not negate the unique power of its original radiance. The modesty of the relays does not necessarily abolish the grandeur of the source. On the contrary. It may be that there was something unique and definitively self-sufficient about Moses, rendering the appearance of any new 'Moses', whether called Jesus, Muhammad or Joseph Smith, superfluous and (to say the very least) suspect.[6]

We are invited by the opening words of the tractate of Fathers to seek this 'something' elsewhere than in the sound and fury of the biblical narrative. Elsewhere than in the 'signs' and 'wonders' that the Lord charged his prophet 'to do in the land of Egypt to Pharaoh, and to all his servants, and to all his land'. Elsewhere than in 'all that mighty hand, and in all the great terror which Moses shewed in the sight of Israel', with whose evocation the Pentateuch closes (Deut 34:11–12).

Moses the liberator and performer of miracles? Is that the most important thing about him? This question is settled unequivocally by the Haggadah – the 'narration' of the escape from slavery in Egypt ritually read every Passover Seder around the Jewish family table – by means of silence. The name of Moses only appears in it once, almost surreptitiously.[7] As if Moses, strangely written off, had simply not been present.

The sole liberator of Israel, the only true author of the 'mighty' miracles that accompanied this liberation, is of course God, and no one else. Neither angel nor messenger features in this affair, the doing of God alone; God, who, if he tasked Moses with leading his people for a time, did not permit him to see his mission through, requiring him (to his chagrin) to hand over to another – Joshua – who would finish the work.

While the Haggadah, despite the Bible and almost contrary to it, implicitly tells us what the greatness of the prophet does *not* consist in, the first four words of the tractate of Fathers suggest where it might reside: 'Moses received (the) Torah from Sinai.'

Moses is the only one who is said to have received (the) Torah from Sinai. Of the ensuing figures (Joshua, Elders, Prophets, members of the Great Assembly), it is only said that they 'transmitted'. As for those who came later still, while the opening chapter of the tractate of Fathers specifies that they 'received', it is only in order to retrace the history of an ordinary transmission: a master is only ever the disciple of an earlier master. Moses receives (the) Torah from Sinai and, prior to Sinai, there is nothing.

It is not the Torah that accounts for the greatness of Moses, but the quality of his reception of it. He is the first and only one who, without any mediation, draws directly from the very fount of divine science. While God appears to other prophets 'in a vision [*mar'ah*]', or makes himself known to them 'in a dream', such is the not the case with Moses (Num 12:6). 'With him will I speak mouth to mouth [*peh el-peh*] ', says God of Moses, '[in a clear vision] (*mar'eh*), and not in dark speeches' (Num 12:8). If this passage, in which God himself characterizes Moses's prophecy, curiously seems a little lacking in clarity here and there, it is nevertheless of clarity that it speaks.

Revelation does not come to Moses in dreams, which means that it does not come to him in images or in sleep. Moses the prophet is a wakeful prophet, never a sleeper, and not a dreamer. This is something that medieval Jewish philosophers spelt out in their own terms: for Moses the outpouring of divine truths did not proceed via the intermediary – obligatory for all other prophets – of the 'imaginative faculty', the corporeal faculty whose action commonly consists in preserving the memory of sensible things, combining them and retracing their images; and which in sleep, benefiting from the repose of the senses, is open to the inspiration of true dreams or prophecy. Only Moses, Maimonides* tells us, while awake and via his rational faculty alone, could access an intelligible perception of truth that was clear and pure; for this reason, only he could enjoin the Law on Israel.[8] Purity and transparency of divine communication is exclusive to Moses. Rashi will put it more plainly: 'I explain my words to him in the clearest form and I do not conceal them in mysteries.' No allegories, no riddles, no rebuses. The revelation of a Law – by definition exacting and precise – obviously cannot afford to take the risk of such detours. Everything is said, clearly stated and clearly perceived; and thereafter, in principle, clearly transmitted. This may be why God presents his 'face-to-face' with Moses in rather peculiar terms in the passage from Numbers. He mentions not 'face to face' but 'mouth to mouth', perhaps in order to signify that what God's mouth has clearly said to Moses, and which Moses has clearly perceived, cannot then but be faultlessly transmitted to Israel by Moses's 'mouth'.

What 'mouth to mouth' denotes is thus clarity of transmission. The face-to-face in the strict sense, underlining the proximity and intimacy of the relationship, is not forgotten. The phrase *panim el-panim* – literally 'face to face' this time – is in fact used elsewhere to characterize the relationship between God and Moses. Thus Deuteronomy 34:10, where Moses is presented as the only one 'whom the Lord knew face to face'. Or, again, in Exodus 33:11: 'And the Lord spake unto Moses face to face, as a man speaketh unto his friend.' So, everything seems to be for the best. I say it seems that way. For if the idea of a 'mouth-to-mouth' between God and his prophet became established without much apparent difficulty, such was not the case with 'face-to-face'. That Moses can hear his God presents no problem. That he might also see him does not stand to reason, if I can put it like that. Numbers 12:8 seems explicit, however: 'the image of the Lord shall he [Moses – and he alone] behold'. What? Like others, Rashi is disturbed by the formula and corrects it. As we know, Moses was only ever able to see God from behind. No doubt he asked (and hoped) for more the day he said: 'shew me thy glory' (Exod 33:18). But God was clear: 'Thou canst not see my face: for there shall no man see me, and live . . . thou shalt see my back parts: but my face shall not be seen' (Exod 33:20–23). So, if a 'face-to-face' did take place via a clear and distinct vision, it was doubtless only that once, and even then, it was actually a 'face-to-back'.

Of course, even with Moses, the symmetry is misleading. We can thus understand why God is always the subject of the verb: it is he who knows Moses 'face to face' (Deut 34:10), not vice versa, and he who speaks to Moses 'face to face' (Exod 33:11), not vice versa. What is more, in the latter case, it is the quality of the communication that is prioritized (God is speaking to Moses), not that of a possibly visual 'face-to-face'. After all, must we always see one another in order to understand each other clearly? And do the proximity and intimacy of a relationship necessarily involve sight? This is far from certain. To say 'face to face' in connection with Moses is just another way of repeating 'mouth to mouth'. In both cases, it can only be a 'manner of speaking' – and this in two senses. On the one hand, it is a formula, an image, a way of presenting things. On the other, it merely evokes the close, transparent way in which these two (God and Moses) communicated, without intermediary, without mediation,[9] informally even: Moses 'was intimate with him and spoke to him whenever he wished'.[10]

In fact, how could a 'face-to-face' in the strict sense ever be what differentiated Moses from other prophets, since prior to him another already fancied he could pride himself on such a relationship? After his struggle with the Angel, does not Jacob say: 'I have seen God face to face, and my life is preserved' (Gen 32:30)? Perhaps it was not really God (as evidence, Jacob did not die), or not really 'face-to-face'. If Moses must absolutely be set above all other prophets not only by the clarity of his hearing, but also by the clarity of a vision and the sublimity of a face-to-face, then this superiority can only be defined negatively. All other prophets imagined themselves seeing the face of God. While seeing, Moses knew it was not the face of God that he saw.[11] So if there is a Mosaic 'exception', it is to be sought in this absolute clarity of a vision that was not a vision. Seeing more than any man could see; seeing, unlike all other prophets, through a glass (or in a mirror) that was clear and clean,[12] Moses knew he was not seeing. If there is a Mosaic 'exception', it is to be sought in this half-blind 'face-to-face' and Moses's acute, perfect consciousness of its imperfection.

A Face and Its Veil

Moses's own face attests to the intensity – as well as the ambiguity – of this 'face-to-face' with its unique, utterly distinctive character: 'And it came to pass, when Moses came down from mount Sinai with the two tables* of testimony in Moses's hand, when he came down from the mount, that Moses wist not that the skin of his face shone while he talked with him' (Exod 34:29).

From his 'face-to-face' or 'mouth-to-mouth' interview with the Lord, Moses emerges literally transfigured. He does not know it (or not yet), but others perceive it. This transfiguration frightens Aaron and all the children of Israel, who dare not come near him. There have been many comments of the term that describes the change in him (*karan*), which might equally imply that Moses came down from the mountain wearing horns. Snide observers have even suggested that the transfiguration was simply a painful disfigurement, the result of not having drunk or eaten anything for forty days and forty nights. The skin of his face had simply 'shrivelled up' (became hard and dry like horn). In fact, the great majority of interpreters, Jews as well as Christians, believe that Moses's face – or, more precisely, 'the skin of his face' – shone at this point; and that it was this radiance that so terrified a people seeing its prophet again for the first time after an absence of forty days.[13]

At the antipodes of any 'horned' or 'animalistic' reading of Exodus 34:29, which is necessarily unsettling, the 'luminist' interpretation of Moses's transfiguration, in addition to the fact that it is almost unanimous, possesses several advantages. It enables us – and this is not insignificant for a commentator – to raise some subtle questions. What kind of light surrounds the face of the prophet? What is its source? What does it mean? Why is it said to shine only on Moses's second descent from Sinai and during the conferral of the second Tables? And why does this radiance inspire fear in those who witness it?

For Maimonides, the phenomenon evidently refers to the specificity of Moses's prophecy: 'We are like someone in a very dark night over whom lightning flashes time and time again. Among us there is one for whom the lightning flashes time and time again, so that he is always, as it were, in unceasing light. Thus night appears to him as day. That is the degree of the great one among the prophets.'[14] For mystics, Moses's face shines with the original light with which God had enlightened the first man, thanks to which the latter saw from one end of the world to the other, and which then God had to conceal so that the guilty generations could not enjoy it, and which he finally restored to his prophet on Sinai.[15]

A spiritual rather than a physical light, a gift of second sight and higher wisdom, the brilliance of Moses's face has its source in God himself. The Midrashic and related literature on the subject is long-winded on this score and medieval commentators do not fail to draw on it: Moses shines because God placed his hand on him to shield him during the passage of his Glory (Exod 33:22); he shines from the sparks that fell from the mouth of the divine Presence as he taught him the Torah; he shines from the radiance of the Tables themselves, written by the finger of God; finally, he shines from having wiped in the hair of his forehead the excess ink from the pen with which he took down the Torah at God's dictation. And Bahya* ben Asher recalls, as if to wrap up this compendium, a verse from Ecclesiastes (8:1) that is indeed very apt: 'A man's wisdom maketh his face to shine, and the boldness of his face shall be changed.'

This unanimous 'glorification' of Moses is not only intended to highlight profound, hidden realities, naturally exciting a sacred fear. It also, and perhaps above all, seeks to defend him. Thus, in his commentary on the Pentateuch written around 1240, Hezekia ben Manoah stresses one of the underlying purposes of this miraculous radiance. The bestowal of the first Tables, he explains, occurred publicly and in a blaze of super-natural manifestations. By contrast, the second are handed to Israel after a private, secret encounter between God and Moses. The extraordinary brilliance of Moses's face is there to authenti-cate this second mission – not only in the eyes of Israel itself, but also, of course, in the eyes of any nations that might have been tempted 'to open their mouths' and challenge it.[16]

However, the biblical account itself is more equivocal than it appears. Moses certainly shines. He invites Aaron, the community leaders and, finally, Israel as a whole to overcome their fear and approach him, so that he can convey 'all that the Lord has spoken with him in mount Sinai' (Exod 34:32). But here is how the text proceeds:

> Moses, [having] done speaking with them, put a veil on his face (33). But when Moses went in before the Lord to speak with him, he took the veil off, until he came out. And he came out, and spake unto the children of Israel that which he was commanded (34). And the children of Israel saw the face of Moses, that the skin of Moses's face shone: and Moses put the veil upon his face again, until he went in to speak with him (35).

We no more escape ambiguity on this occasion than on others: Moses shines, certainly, but he also veils himself. When he is no longer in God's presence, once he has finished conveying to Israel the teachings communicated to him by God, and after Israel has clearly seen that his face is shining, the prophet conceals his face behind a veil which he removes only during his next interview with the Lord. But why does Moses conceal his face? And what exactly is he hiding? What, fundamentally, is signified by the advent of a screen where once there was only transparency, of a shade where once all was light?

For fledgling Christianity, the opportunity was too good to miss. And it did not fail to seize it. Thus the patristic interpretation of Exodus 34:29–35 was largely influenced by the exegesis in II Corinthians 3:6–18. If the glory of 'the ministration of death, written and engraven in stones', was such that the Hebrews could not behold Moses's face, how much more glorious will 'the ministration of the spirit' be! Moses veiled himself only so 'that the children of Israel could not steadfastly look to the end of that which is abolished'. And to this day there 'remaineth the same veil' over the eyes of their descendants and successors (the Jews), obscuring their understanding of the Ancient Law itself. This veil has not been lifted for them, since it 'is done away in Christ' and him alone. Paul insists that 'even unto this day, when Moses is read, the veil is upon their heart.' Only to Christians, whose face has been uncovered, there now falls the privilege of reflecting the glory of the Lord.

Christianity – Israel in spirit – will in fact recuperate two symbols, to its own advantage and the detriment of Judaism and carnal Israel. First, that of the veil, referring to the blindness of the Jews, which will be concretely associated with medieval Christian representations of the Synagogue. Next, that of the transfiguration – incomplete and temporary in Moses, complete and definitive in – and through – Jesus. The exegesis by Origen (c. 185–c. 254) already, and eloquently,[17] linked Exodus 34:29–35 to Gospel accounts of Jesus's transfiguration: 'And after six days Jesus taketh Peter, James, and John his brother, and bringeth them up into an high mountain apart, And was transfigured before them: and his face did shine as the sun, and his raiment was white as the light. And, behold, there appeared unto them Moses and Elijah talking with him' (Matt 17:1–3).[18] The 'high mountain' has replaced Sinai. Peter, James and John, witnesses of the miracle, have replaced Israel. And it is Jesus whose face now shines. Not only his face, moreover, but all of him, the miraculous brilliance extending to his clothes.

Moses is there, alongside Elijah, as if to register his defeat. And Moses and he together speak with Jesus. Just as Moses once spoke with his God? Highly impressed, Peter suggests to Jesus that they put up three tents, one for each of the three characters. Not worth it. A bright cloud covers them and, from within it, a voice designates Jesus as 'my beloved Son, in whom I am well pleased' (Matt 17:5). No sooner do the disciples raise their eyes than standing before them is 'Jesus only' (Matt 17:8). There is no veil in this story, just the total (and definitive?) eclipse of Elijah and, especially, of Moses.

While not altogether hopeless, the matter is a serious one and no Jewish commentator can avoid confronting it. So, what are we to make of the veil with which Moses covers his face? For we have to make something of it. Christians compel us to – possibly more than the letter of the text itself does. Behind this veil, once it has fallen, does Moses's face still shine? Or has its brilliance faded? What is Moses concealing: a face that has reverted to its everyday dullness, or a face that shines on? For some – for most – only one choice is possible: Moses's face continues to shine behind its veil. Its radiance is never dulled, precisely what is suggested by Deuteronomy 34:7, assuring us that to the day he died 'his eye was not dim, nor his natural force abated'. Why, then, should this light be veiled between two revelations? Lest the brilliance, which remains somewhat disconcerting and even a little scary, upset the Hebrews appearing before the prophet charged with settling their disputes: they might lose their faculties and forget their arguments.[19] Or – another option – 'out of respect for the rays of majesty, lest all enrich themselves from it';[20] 'out of respect for this light which God maintained on his face, so that Israel could not see it at any time, but only when he conveyed the words of the Lord to them'.[21]

Thus Moses veiled his face to avoid trivializing the divine light shining through him and to reserve the spectacle for circumstances justifying it. He lifted his veil in the presence of God, when he talked with him, and that is normal: for the 'face-to-face' to occur – the 'face-to-face' with which Moses is the only prophet ever to be graced – any screen must obviously disappear. Even more interesting: the veil was also raised at the moment of another face-to-face – that of Moses with his people, when he communicates what God has taught him. No veil, then, no screen, nothing that masks, nothing that disturbs. On the contrary, a pure light, diffused unchecked, at the two key moments in the reception/transmission of the Law: when Moses receives the Torah from Sinai and when he transmits it to Israel. The essential thing is preserved: the unsullied transparency of perfect communication. No veil between Israel and the 'Old Covenant', and no eclipse either. On the contrary, the veil falls only to protect a light that never dims, which on each unveiling still has its original brilliance and power in the eyes of those who contemplate it. The veil is only there to stop the Hebrews having eyes and soul that have grown too 'accustomed'. At the end of the day it is merely the veil that separates, as it must, the sacred from the profane.

So, for a Jewish reader, Jesus and his cloud cannot in any way dim the prophet's brilliance or obscure the absolute limpidity – for Israel and Israel only, since Israel alone saw the veil lifted whenever necessary – of what he has transmitted. This being the case, is the possible dimming of the brilliance of Moses's face under this veil, in between two episodes of reception/transmission of the Law, really as troubling as we imagine? Is it really so important to deny it? What matters in the first instance is the perfection of the communication between God, Moses and

Israel; and it is ensured, whatever else happens: the veil falls only when this communication is suspended. The celestial voice that resounds from the cloud to confirm Jesus in his mission should not impress us any more than that. Ever since Moses, after all, ever since the Torah was transmitted by him to us, and transmitted in its entirety, have we not known that the Torah is no longer up in heaven, but down here below? 'It is not in heaven, that thou shouldest say, Who shall go up for us to heaven, and bring it unto us, that we may hear it, and do it?' (Deut 30:12). The time of prophecy has long passed. No one can now rely on a private divine revelation to impose his point of view; no miracle, not even a 'voice' from Heaven, can authenticate the slightest teaching; and pending issues are now resolved by majority. God himself has adjusted to this idea. He positively rejoices over his defeat, repeating with a smile: 'My sons have vanquished me, my sons have vanquished me'.[22] Have Jesus, his luminous cloud, and the 'voice' that emerges from it sufficed to make us doubt all that, spurring us, rather hastily perhaps, to credit Moses unnecessarily with continuous radiance even behind his veil?

The light is not in the face of the prophet, but in the Torah he has revealed. The light of the prophet's face might well fade on occasion; that of the Law remains intact. And if the prophet exposes his shining face only when he receives and transmits the Law, it is so as to make it perfectly clear (if I dare say) that this light is attached to the Law, and to nothing else. His face, in between two moments of revelation, might well lose its brilliance and revert to its ordinary state. And if he conceals this temporary fading behind a veil, it is only out of consideration for folk 'bereft of reason',[23] who, in that generation of little faith and adoring a Golden Calf, might have drawn erroneous conclusions. We cannot help the fact that Christians of more recent generations sometimes fall for them. But what have we got to lose by conceding to Moses this additional evidence of his humanity: the temporary fading of his brilliance? Is there not instead a lot to gain? Moses, the greatest prophet Israel has ever known, remains a man.

Moses and Khidr

When the veil is lifted and his face shines, Moses is indeed the greatest prophet Israel has ever known. He is 'our master', '*Rabbenu*', in the standard formula, instructed in his Law by God himself, and instructing us in it in turn, in the purity and transparency of an absolute, unveiled transmission. But when the veil falls, Moses is himself again, 'the man Moses'. His veil conceals and reveals this limitation to us: Moses's sheer humanity. Behind his veil, Moses resembles us again. The desert generation – that of the rebellions – doubtless had to ignore it (or see it as little as possible). But we, surely, can face it, can't we? Over the course of this book, we have been able to recognize behind the veil the wounded body of the prophet, the son of the Egyptian woman, the one stalked by death in the night of the journey, the woman, and the ultimate victim of divine obscure entrapments; behind his veil, we have been able to recognize and delineate the plain face of a plainly human Moses, frail and uncertain. But does all this mean that Moses was less than he should have been? Would a frail Moses be a diminished Moses? Does the lack – '*gera'on*', Abraham Ibn Ezra would have said[24] – we have allowed ourselves to recognize in him truly detract from him?

For its part, Islam seemingly has no problem with Moses's greatness. Sufism regards him as a master of initiation into the Way. In the Qur'an, he is the most cited of the prophets who precede Muhammad: 136 occasions. And for good reason: he is also the prophet whose 'mission and trajectory' most closely resemble those of the founder of Islam.[25] Allah addresses him as follows: 'Moses, I have raised you above other people by [giving you] my messages and speaking to you' (7:144). Moreover Allah claims to have created Moses 'for [him]self', 'under [his] watchful eye',[26] 'shower[ing] [him] with love' (20:39, 41). Yet even though Moses's grandeur (his virtual perfection) is thus established and clearly affirmed, the Qur'an also depicts Moses in a curious story where he does not come off well. In it he is no longer a teacher, but a pupil, and a poor one at that: talkative, impatient, and incapable of seeing beyond the surface of things.

In the course of a mysterious journey undertaken with his own disciple, Moses comes across an enigmatic character, whose name the Qur'an does not mention, but whom the Muslim tradition recognizes as Khidr, also called 'the Verdant', because wherever he is he causes nature to become lush and green. Having drunk at the source of Life, he has become immortal; he is the initiator of the prophets and saints, defying the limits of space and time. In many of his features, Khidr recalls the prophet Elijah of Jewish popular legends.[27] The Qur'an simply presents him thus: 'One of Our servants, a man to whom We had granted Our mercy and whom We had given knowledge of Our own' (18:65). Moses wishes to follow him and become his disciple, to be instructed by him in at least part of the 'right guidance' in which Khidr himself has been instructed (18:66). This master – who, need it be said, is not God – knows things that Moses does not know. For his part, Khidr hesitates: will Moses be capable of the kind of patience such an apprenticeship requires? Moses assures him he will, but Khidr guessed right. On witnessing the seemingly outrageous acts perpetrated by Khidr during their journey, Moses proves unable to hold his tongue or check his impatience. Khidr sinks a boat they get into, kills a young man, and repairs a tumbledown wall inside a town where they have been refused hospitality. On each occasion Moses grows agitated and indignant, and wonders noisily what is going on. This behaviour reveals him to be the bad disciple his master had predicted. Khidr therefore dismisses him, after explaining the reasons for actions that were only apparently shocking. He ends their interview with these words: 'I did not do [these things] of my own accord: these are the explanations for those things which you could not bear with patience' (18:82). It must be said that the justifications adduced by Khidr are not that convincing. He supposedly sank the vessel to protect its penniless owners from the rapacity of a pirate king; killed the young man because he was destined to become impious, and Providence would confer on his faithful parents a new and worthier offspring; as to the wall which he repaired, it concealed a treasure that two orphans, children of a righteous man, would discover on coming of age. It does not matter if we find these explanations questionable. For it is not so much Khidr as Moses who interests us. Now, the Moses shown here is a disciple, not a master, a plain man who wants to understand, but does not understand, and loses his temper – with Khidr and, above and beyond him, with God – before the misfortune of the innocent and the good fortune of the wicked. If Moses is the man we think he is, he is unlikely to be content with the responses of such as Khidr. And though he is rendered more 'knowledgeable' by the latter's revelations, this newly acquired 'science' may be insufficient to dispel his indignation.

This Moses, this apparently mediocre disciple incapable of lifting (or completely lifting) the double veil of scandal and ignorance by himself, is also surprisingly present in the rabbinical tradition.

Moses and Rabbi Akiba

This is what Rav Judah reports in the name of Rav (third century):

> When Moses went up to heaven, he found the Holy One, blessed be his name, seated and engaged in attaching crowns to the letters [of the Torah]. He said to him: 'Master of the universe, who is staying your hand?' [God] answered him: 'A man will come at the end of several generations by the name of Akiba, son of Joseph, who will draw mountains of laws from each detail [of the text]. [Moses] said to him: 'Master of the universe, show me [this man]!' [God] answered him: 'Turn back!' Moses went to sit [in Rabbi Akiba's class] behind eight rows [of his disciples], and did not understand what they were saying. His strength declined. But when [Rabbi Akiba] came to a certain thing, his disciples said to him: 'Master, where do you get that from?' And [Rabbi Akiba] replied: 'It is a law given to Moses on Sinai!'[28] The spirit [of Moses] was calmed by this. [Moses] turned from them to find the Holy One, blessed be his name, and said to him: 'Master of the universe, you have a man like that, and you impart the Torah through me?' [God] replied: 'Be silent. Thus have I decided!'[29]

For the duration of a brief visit, Moses becomes the pupil of a second-century Jewish teacher, Rabbi Akiba. He humbly sits in the last row, far from the master and behind all his disciples. And he understands nothing of what is said – which comes as no

surprise to us twenty-first-century historians. From Moses to
Rabbi Akiba, how many generations have succeeded one another?
Many. Little wonder that after so many centuries, in Judea under
Roman domination after the destruction of the Second Temple,
and after so many masters and disciples have passed the baton
on, things might be said about the Torah that its original transmitter – if he ever existed – finds himself unable to understand.
History, changing times and contexts, the evolution of language
itself – these are enough to render this poignant denouement
predictable. It is only natural, in such circumstances, that Moses
was felt discouraged – or, to put it like our text, that 'his strength
decline[d]'. This phrase, which we have encountered before,[30]
fits in well here. In other circumstances, readers will remember,
the man Moses had become as 'weak' as a woman. Here, the
quintessential master suddenly appears as 'weak' as the most
ignorant of disciples.

But is that what the story means? Is it simply an implicit
confession? Is it the indirect recognition, perhaps ironic or
vaguely disenchanted, of an undeniable historical fact: that
Israel's Torah, especially its oral Torah, was not 'revealed' in its
entirety on Sinai after all, and what is included under this rubric
is the continuously evolving product of a tradition of instruction
constantly enriched over the centuries, and delivered in very
different socio-historical contexts? Nothing could be less certain.
For this account may not, perhaps, decisively retract the original
assertion, via the tractate of Fathers, of total revelation and transparent transmission: 'Moses received (the) Torah from Sinai, and
transmitted it to Joshua, and Joshua transmitted it to the Elders,
the Elders to the Prophets, and the Prophets to the members of
the Great Assembly.' At most, it qualifies it. Does not Rabbi
Akiba himself offer assurances that the seemingly new (hence

incomprehensible to Moses) instruction he delivers to his own disciples is nonetheless 'a law given to Moses on Sinai'? Does he simply mean that Moses transmitted everything without understanding everything, without having taken the proper measure of the transmitted totality? That he also transmitted the 'crowns' attached by God to the letters of the Torah without grasping what lay behind these very minor details in the way of science and truth? And that the successive generations of masters and disciples, from Moses down to us, served only to reveal what was concealed, to bring what was in germ to blossom, to realize bit by bit the potential of a Revelation which remained hidden to Moses himself?

Perhaps so. But what does it matter in the end? For what matters here is Moses and his frailty, which is once again illustrated. A frailty he himself acknowledges, and which makes him or reveals him to be, again, fundamentally modest: 'Master of the universe,' he exclaims, 'you have a man like him [Rabbi Akiba], and you impart the Torah through me?' To which God replies as he sees fit, by refusing to respond: 'Be silent! Thus have I decided.' Impatient Moses, asking too many questions . . . In fact, he does not stop there. For the story continues:

> [Moses] said to him: 'You have shown me his Torah [the science of Rabbi Akiba]. Show me his salary.' [God] answered him: 'Turn around.' [Moses] turned around and saw that the flesh [of Rabbi Akiba] was being sold by weight in the market. He said to him: 'Such is the Torah, and such is [therefore] his salary?' [God] answered him: 'Be silent. Thus have I decided!'

According to some legends, Rabbi Akiba died at the same age as Moses: 120.[31] But hardly in the same way: he died as a martyr of the Romans – outrageous misfortune of the righteous master. The impatient Moses is forever asking questions. But here again he will obtain no answer. At least in this rabbinical tale God does not bother with convoluted, and ultimately unconvincing, explanations à la Khidr. This time, the veil will not be lifted. No light will come to pierce the darkness. Moses will not learn why God chose him, rather than Rabbi Akiba, to transmit the Torah to Israel and the world. Nor will he learn why Rabbi Akiba, a righteous master, must die a martyr's death. Thus, there are things that Moses will not know. Any more than we do. Despite everything, however great the prophet, some things are not revealed to him. However great the pupil, some things will not be taught him. And however great the master, there are some things that he will never be able to teach us. Because he does not know them.

God twice expels Moses, the stammering prophet, into the absolute of silence. He consigns him to silence. The rationale for the best – revelation of the Torah via Moses – will not be revealed. Any more than the rationale for the worst: the suffering of the righteous master. Twice God says to Moses: 'Be silent!' And Moses is silent, leaving us this silence as a disturbing legacy. But in this silence there perhaps still resonates for us, frail human beings of this generation, muffled but audible, the echo of the frail prophet's final lesson: 'You may well believe in him, but you will not understand him. And even if you do not believe in him, you will not escape the absurdity of his decrees.'

Conclusion

The Moses of this book is not Moses, assuming there ever was a Moses. He is not the Moses of history, or even of Scripture. Without being arbitrary, the portrait I have sketched is certainly incomplete and only relatively coherent. I have liberally derived almost as much in the way of materials, forms and colours from the rabbinical tradition as from the Bible. And, in opting to rely on some of the most enigmatic verses of the scriptural text to clarify his features, and sometimes also to obscure them, I am not unaware that I might have conveyed a sense of hanging 'mountains on a hair'.[1] I take responsibility for these limitations, this presumption and uncertainty. Yes, my Moses is 'frail' in this sense as well.

The Moses of this book is hardly more than one possible Moses. By that I mean an audible Moses: a Moses who speaks to me and, I dare hope, to us all. A Moses conceived, if I may put it like this, in accordance with the *Zeitgeist*. At a time when the Lord barely makes himself heard, when even the 'still small voice' (I K 19:12) that Elijah could still perceive[2] – a 'small' prophecy mysteriously composed of words and silences[3] – when even this frail voice seems to be extinguished, snuffed out by the clamour of the new religious fanatics. A Moses conceived in accordance with the spirit of our time, then, or, more precisely, against the spirit of our time. Because if the Moses of this book speaks to us, he also testifies against us in the end.

In our day, Jews only seem to be able to choose between two Judaisms: that of Abraham, father of the nation, and that of Joshua, conqueror of the Land. On one side, a purely ethnic Judaism, a Judaism of ancestors real or imagined, the Judaism of a community rooted in a line, authentic and closed, asserting against all others a principle of absolute distinction, of strict difference, forgetting that its forebears, assuming they were ever identifiable, were merely 'wandering Arameans',[4] and Abraham, the first of them, a simple convert. On the other side, a Judaism of combat, the idolatry of a Land but above all of a state, its army, its conquests, and identification with all the Joshuas of our times – as if, dreaming of something else, Jews had not ceased to tread this ground for centuries, and as if so many of them did not prefer, even today, the deserts of Exile to the milk and honey of a remote Judea.

Faced with these blood Judaisms – blood of ancestors or blood of battles – I can only discern one other: the Judaism of Moses, the only one that can speak to Jews and non-Jews alike, encompass in its vision both Jews and non-Jews. A Judaism of the spirit, of wandering and incompletion; virtually a Judaism of failure. For Moses failed. He is not the ancestor of any line; his sons disappeared without a trace. The people he led for forty years does not owe its existence to him, but at most its underlying identity. Perhaps it owes him nothing at all. Moses was but an instrument: the instrument of a liberation willed by God and then of the transmission of a Torah imparted by God. He was not even the instrument of the conquest of the Land; he stopped before that, perished before that, reluctantly making way for Joshua. When Moses balks at taking the lead of a whole people to be conducted out of Egypt, God compels him. When the burden is too heavy and his strength fails him and he wants to give up, to die, God does not give way. But when he begs to enter the Holy Land, his Lord refuses him. And to kill him – something he attempts more than once – God finally ensnares him shamelessly, with Moses dying as a sinner.

Do we know at least who Moses is? Of good birth, and yet abandoned and adopted. A Hebrew, an Egyptian, a mere man, sometimes like a woman. A 'man of God', but not a God. A prophet, but with a stammer. A liberator, but not a messiah, and certainly not a Christ. A legislator, but to a people still lacking Land and State. A leader, yes, a soldier, no. A politician, perhaps, but a visionary one. And a servant of the Book. A negotiator, an intercessor, a simple believer at prayer. Powerful, but wielding fragile power. A teacher, yes, and the greatest, but a disciple too, and the most modest. Moses as a model? A model of contradictions, for sure, a model of uncertainty, a model of incompletion.

Moses, that uncertain prophet and true prophet, died in exile. A genuine prophet always dies in exile. That is the clinching sign of his greatness. His gaze, which remains undimmed, always reaches to a horizon he will never set foot in. Israel's greatest ever prophet never entered the Promised Land. Everyone knows this, everyone says it, but many forget what it means: to be great, incomparably so, this prophet had to die in exile. Well, he could hardly become the short-sighted prime minister of an over-armed micro-state imprisoned behind its walls. It was doubly a death in exile, moreover, since the site of Moses's sepulchre is still unknown today. And his lost remains will never be transferred to Jerusalem. He thus spares us innumerable pointless genuflections and dubious prostrations. We shall never light a candle on his tomb. A rare elegance. An obligation for us to go into the heart of the matter.

Moses ceased to be a prophet on the day of his death. Just as God himself ceased to dictate his Law to us once he had revealed the Torah, which is now (as we know) no longer in Heaven where we could ask someone to go and fetch it for us. Though he is no more our prophet, Moses has remained 'our Master', undoubtedly the greatest, but also the humblest: just the first in a long line from which we all ultimately descend. Yes, Joshua, the military man, was his first successor. But note this! When God asked Moses to transfer his burden to Joshua, by laying his hand on him, he expressed himself quite clearly: 'Thou shalt put some of thine [majesty] upon him' (Num 27:20). What is this majesty? The 'shining' skin of Moses's face, if we are to believe the Targum. And was this majesty transferred in its entirety? No: it is not written 'thou shall put thine majesty', but 'thou shalt put *some* of thine majesty'. Or, as an old rabbinical teaching has it, 'Moses's face was like the sun, and that of Joshua like the moon'.[5] Joshua isn't quite as great.

The modesty of the man Moses is simply the other side of his grandeur. It is the recognition by the greatest among us of the insuperable imperfection that makes him unquestionably a man. The modesty of Moses the pupil of the Midrash is simply the other side of the grandeur of the master of Scripture. The best homage we can render him is perhaps to forget about Moses, the great Moses, and simply, modestly, learn from him and, by making ourselves small, have the chance to one day achieve a semblance of grandeur. Renouncing the pride of the 'race', the violence of arms and the tyranny of Place, whoever we are, let us likewise sit somewhere behind the eighth row of disciples. Perhaps this is the 'Judaism of Moses'. Receiving and transmitting. Listening, even when the message is confused. Questioning, sometimes insistently, even when there is no answer. And inventing, yes, as and when necessary. So what does a 'Judaism of Moses' come down to? Neither a DNA, nor an army, nor a territory, but quite simply a school, where some faces, childlike or otherwise, occasionally shine with a strange brilliance: that of a joyous science.

Glossary and Biographical Notes

Ahad Ha'am

In Hebrew literally 'one of the people', pen name of Asher Zvi Hirsch Ginsberg, a Hebrew writer and theoretician of cultural Zionism (Skvyra, Russia, 1856–Tel Aviv, 1927). Born into a Hassidic family, following a traditional education, as a very young man he was attracted by the Haskalah (the Jewish Enlightenment movement). Prior to immigration into Palestine and the creation of a political entity, he advocated the renaissance of a secular, Hebrew Jewish culture, with that country destined to become a spiritual centre of influence over the whole Jewish world. To this end, he created the semi-clandestine organization *Bnei Mosheh* ('Sons of Moses') in 1889, founded a publishing house in Odessa in 1896, and edited the Zionist Hebrew-language organ *Ha-Shiloah* (*The Messenger*). He emigrated to Palestine in 1922. He was one of the few Zionists of the time to be aware of the existence of an Arab question. His writings have been collected in English under the title *Essays, Letters, Memoirs* (1946).

Bahya ben Asher

Author (c. 1260–1340) of a very popular commentary on the Pentateuch, which was the first Kabbalistic book ever printed (1492). In it, registering the inherent polysemy of the scriptural text, he developed a quadruple approach: the way of the *pshat* (literal meaning); that of the *midrash* (homiletic meaning); that of the *sekhel* (the 'intellect' – reason or philosophy); and that of the *sod* (the 'secret' or Kabbalah).

Covenant

In Hebrew *brit*. Scripture refers to four main covenants – the first between God and Noah, the second and third between God and Abraham, and the fourth between God and Israel. Heralded on the eve of the Flood (Gen 6:18), the covenant with Noah is sealed after he – the one righteous man of his generation – has escaped general annihilation in the ark (Gen 9:8-17). God promises Noah and his progeny never to unleash another flood. The establishment of this covenant, whose sign is the rainbow, is significantly preceded in Genesis by the formulation of a charter to govern the relations between human beings and the natural world, as well as between human beings (Gen 9:1–7). Rabbinical Judaism would base its definition of the basic legal code of the Seven Laws of Noah on this passage. This initial model, associating the covenant with the law, is found once more in the subsequent covenant that specifically unites God with Israel. It is heralded and prepared by the covenant between God and Abraham. In Genesis 15, God promises the patriarch whom he has 'brought . . . out of Ur of the Chaldees' (Gen 15:7) numerous descendants, born of Sarah, who after a period of exile and oppression will inherit the land he has brought him to. This covenant is sealed by a ceremony during which 'a smoking furnace, and a burning lamp' (Gen 15:17) pass between the pieces of the animals slaughtered by Abraham (hence its name *brit bein ha-betarim*, literally 'covenant of the pieces').

In Genesis 17, renewing his pledge of 'an everlasting covenant' (verse 7), God asks Abraham and his posterity to observe the ritual of circumcision as a token of loyalty to this covenant. The collective, public covenant made by God and Israel during the theophany on Sinai (Exodus 19) is at once the confirmation, renewal and deepening of the Abrahamic covenant. The patriarch's descendants, whom the experience of slavery and exodus has formed into a nation, freely enters into a covenant with God. Led by Moses, Israel, wrested from slavery in Egypt and saved from the waters of the Red Sea, undertakes to fulfil the words of the Everlasting God and become 'a kingdom of priests, and an holy nation' (verse 6). In return, God pledges to make it a 'peculiar treasure unto me above all people' (verse 5). The Decalogue and the whole Torah represent the charter of this contract involving the observance by Israel, in addition to exclusive worship, of ethical, social and political rules sanctioned by divine decree. Israel's respect for the terms of the covenant conditions its historical development and its relationship to its land: 'Ye shall walk in all the ways which the Lord your God hath commanded you, that ye may live, and that it may be well with you, and that ye may prolong your days in the land which ye shall possess' (Deut 5:33). This covenant is solemnly sealed in the blood of the sacrifices with which Moses sprinkles the people, saying: 'Behold the blood of the covenant (*dam ha-brit*), which the Lord hath made with you concerning all these words' (Exod 24:8). It is inscribed on the stone of the 'Tablets of the Covenant' (*luhot ha-brit*) kept in the 'Ark of the Covenant' (*aron ha-brit*), which was initially installed in the mobile sanctuary of the desert and then in the holy of holies of the Temple of Jerusalem.

Decalogue, or Ten Commandments

In Hebrew, *aseret ha-devarim* or *aseret ha-dibrot* – literally, 'the ten words' or 'the ten sayings'. Pronounced by God during the theophany

of Sinai and inscribed on the 'Tablets of the Covenant', the
Decalogue – the Covenant's constitutive text – lays down the theological and ethical principles that are to guide Israel's conduct: (1)
exclusive submission to the God who brought the Hebrews out of
Egypt; (2) prohibition of idolatry; (3) prohibition of blasphemy; (4)
observance of the Shabbat; (5) honouring parents; (6) prohibition of
murder; (7) prohibition of adultery; (8) prohibition of theft; (9) prohibition of bearing false witness; and (10) prohibition of covetousness.
The Bible offers two slightly different versions of the text (Exod 20:2–14
and Deut 5:6–18). Despite its significance in Jewish consciousness, and
the interest shown in it by interpreters, the Decalogue has not been
integrated into the everyday liturgy, to forestall any temptation to
establish a hierarchy in Revelation by prioritizing some commandments over others.

Gregory of Nyssa

Born in Cappadocia around 330 and dying in 394, this Greek Father
was the author, *inter alia*, of a *Life of Moses* in two parts. The first,
referred to by the title of *historia*, which involves a strictly literal exegesis, furnishes a summary of the life of the prophet according to Exodus
and Numbers. The second, by far the more important, entitled *theoria*,
reinterprets Moses's life as a symbol of the mystical life of the soul, in
the framework of a spiritual exegesis – a genre inaugurated by Philo
Judaeus of Alexandria.

Ibn Ezra (Abraham)

Biblical exegete, philosopher, poet, grammarian, astrologer, astronomer,
mathematician and physician (1089–1167). Around the age of fifty,
Abraham Ibn Ezra left his native Spain to lead a nomadic existence that
took him to Italy, France and England. A secular and religious poet, he
was a crucial link in the transmission of the Judeo-Arab cultural

heritage to Jewish communities settled in Christian lands, by producing a profuse, diverse oeuvre in Hebrew. Rather neo-Platonist in inspiration, his philosophy is mainly expounded in his commentaries. In fact, it was primarily as a biblical interpreter of remarkable fertility and rigour that he imposed himself on posterity after Rashi. His commentaries, which can be hard going on account of their compressed and often enigmatic style, were read, cited, imitated and themselves the subject of a host of supercommentaries. His method itself was an important milestone. His independence earned him many attacks, but also the respect of Spinoza.

Josephus (Flavius)

From his Hebrew name Yosef Ben Matityahu, military leader and historian (c. 38–100). He first of all participated on the Jewish side in the revolt against Rome that began in 66. Under siege in Jotapata, he 'betrayed' and defected to Vespasian. And it was from the Roman camp that he witnessed the fall of Jerusalem and the destruction of the Temple in 70. Loyal to his faith and his God, as well as Rome, Josephus was the author of two historical works of exceptional interest – *Antiquities of the Jews* and *The Jewish War*. He also wrote an autobiography and a polemical and apologetic text, *Against Apion*.

Kabbalah

From the Hebrew *kabbalah* (literally 'tradition'), the word refers specifically to the mystical tradition in Judaism. Its roots are ancient, as is attested in particular by the literature of the 'Palaces' (*heikhalot*), some of whose documents date back to the third or fourth century. A Jewish pietism influenced by Sufism developed in Spain and Egypt in the eleventh and twelfth centuries, and another pietistic tendency – the 'German Pietists' (*Hasidei Ashkenaz*) between 1150 and 1250 – left a dual legacy, theological and ethical. But it was in

Provence and the Languedoc, and then in Spain, that the Kabbalah proper yielded its first fruits. In the second half of the thirteenth century, two Spaniards enduringly marked this current: Abraham Abulafia, who developed a mysticism of language leading into an ecstatic experience; and Moses de León, who cultivated a theosophical kabbalah whose teachings are to be found in the *Sefer ha-Zohar* (*The Book of Splendour*). From then on, and especially after the expulsion of the Jews from Spain in 1492, the Kabbalah consistently accompanied – and even dominated – the development of Judaism in the Holy Land, with the flourishing Sephardic centre of Safed in the sixteenth century, but also in Eastern Europe with Hassidism from the eighteenth century.

Maimonides (Moses)

Philosopher, jurist, commentator and physician (1138–1204). Born in Spain, active in Egypt, Maimonides left an abundant, polymorphous oeuvre that has profoundly marked the development of rabbinical Judaism. The author of a large number of medical treatises, he originally distinguished himself as a jurist. In addition to a commentary in Arabic on the Mishnah and a *Book of Commandments*, he produced (in Hebrew) a systematic, monumental code of Jewish Law, the *Mishneh Torah* ('Repetition of the Torah', after Deuteronomy 17:18), also known under the title *Yad ha-Hazakah* ('The Strong Hand'). Maimonides was the most eminent representative of medieval Jewish Aristotelianism with his *Guide of the Perplexed*, written in Arabic and rapidly translated into Hebrew.

Midrash

Hebrew term (from the Hebraic root *drsh*, 'to seek', 'to enquire'; plural *midrashim*), referring to classical rabbinical exegesis of Scripture as it developed for the most part in the Holy Land, preserved in a prolific literature that testifies to a rich, active tradition of teaching and preaching. If their composition continued from the fifth to the eleventh centuries in various parts of the diaspora (Palestine, Babylonia, Byzantium, Languedoc, etc.), the major collections of *midrashim*, like the Midrashic developments of the two Talmuds, are evidence of very old traditions.

Mishnah

From the Hebrew, literally 'repetition, teaching'. Codification of the oral Law published around 200. Composed in a distinctive idiom (called Mishnaic Hebrew, different from Biblical Hebrew), in a style at once concise and precise, the Mishnah formulates the Law without always reporting the debates or divergences that have accompanied its history and determined its development, and only rarely signalling the scriptural texts it is based on. The Mishnah comprises six sections or 'orders' (*sedarim*) and sixty-three tractates.

Mizrahi (Elijah)

Born in Constantinople around 1450 and deceased in 1526, rabbinical authority and famous jurist, a mathematician translated into Latin, Mizrahi was the author, *inter alia*, of a supercommentary on Rashi on the Pentateuch, first published in Venice in 1527.

Nachmanides (Moses)

Biblical exegete, Talmudist, Kabbalist and poet (1194–1270). Eminent representative of the Kabbalistic circle of Girona, Nachmanides was a remarkable jurist at the junction of the French and Spanish traditions. In 1262, he was compelled to participate in a public disputation in Barcelona organized by Friar Pablo Christiani in the presence of King James I of Aragon, and provided an account of it in *The Book of the Disputation*. He ultimately had to journey to the Holy Land, where he completed his commentary on the Pentateuch, combining philosophical, Midrashic and Kabbalistic elements.

Pentateuch

The Torah in the strict sense, also called *Humash* – a condensed form of *hamishah humshei Torah* (literally 'the five fifths of the Law') – the Pentateuch comprises the five books whose authorship is attributed by Jewish tradition to Moses. It forms the first set of texts of the scriptural corpus defined by Judaism (it is followed by the Prophets and Hagiographa). These five books – Genesis, Exodus, Leviticus, Numbers and Deuteronomy – successively present the Creation of the world and the Flood, the adventures of the Patriarchs down to the settlement of Jacob's family in Egypt, the slavery in Egypt, the Exodus, the theophany of Sinai and the Covenant, and the wanderings of the Hebrews in the desert until the death of Moses on the eve of their entry into Canaan. Along with narratives, the Pentateuch contains the set of ritual and legal prescriptions that form the armature of biblical religion. It is here that rabbinical Judaism identifies the 613 commandments whose observance is required of Israel, and its legal authority is held by it to be superior to that of all other biblical writings.

Philo of Alexandria

A distinguished representative of Hellenistic Jewish culture, Philo (13 BCE–54 CE) attempted to harmonize the teachings of Judaism with the principles of Greek thought, Platonist and Stoic in particular. A key source of information on the Jewish realities of his time, his oeuvre, composed in Greek, comprises historical, apologetic and philosophical texts, as well as numerous biblical commentaries. It exercised considerable influence on the Church Fathers. By contrast, it remained overlooked by the classical rabbinical tradition.

Rashbam

Acronym of **Ra**bbi **Sh**muel **B**en **M**eir (Rabbi Samuel son of Meir), grandson of Rashi, biblical and Talmudic commentator (c. 1080–85– c. 1174). His biblical exegesis is one of the few in Judaism that can be characterized as literalist in the strict sense.

Rashi

Acronym of **Ra**bbi **Sh**lomo **I**tzhaki (Rabbi Salomon son of Isaac), biblical and Talmudic commentator (1040–1105). Born in Troyes during the reign of Henri I, educated in the great Jewish academies of the time, Rashi returned to his native city to devote himself to teaching. It was there that he produced a virtually complete commentary on the Bible and a commentary on the Babylon Talmud. These commentaries represent a milestone in the history of traditional Jewish exegesis and still form part of the basic education of the faithful today. Moreover, the influence of his biblical commentaries extended well beyond the confines of the Jewish world and, via the *Postillae Perpetuae* of the Franciscan Nicholas of Lyra (c. 1270–1349), who cited them, reached Protestants and the first modern translators of Scripture.

Schoenberg (Arnold)

Austrian Jewish musician (Vienna 1874–Los Angeles 1951). Having converted to Protestantism in 1898, he returned to Judaism in 1933, during a ceremony conducted in private in Paris, in the liberal synagogue on rue Copernic, and emigrated to the United States. His very strong attachment to the Jewish people and its biblical heritage found expression, *inter alia*, in the composition, unfinished at his death, of the opera *Moses and Aaron*.

Shabbat

From the Hebrew, literally 'cessation day' or 'rest day'. Last day of the week in the Jewish calendar, beginning Friday evening at sunset and ending Saturday evening at night. Shabbat commemorates the completion of the work of Creation. It is also associated with the memory of the deliverance from slavery. Rabbinical law rigorously defined and detailed the tasks proscribed during the Shabbat. Released from secular obligations, renouncing his hold on the world, the practising Jew employs the recovered freedom of the Shabbat to strengthen his links with his community, devote himself to his family, and refocus his existence on its spiritual dimension, through prayer and study. Impressing its specific rhythm on Jewish temporality, the Shabbat is not only a day of proscribed activities; it is also, and above all, a day of joy, of pleasure valued and actively sought. It prefigures and heralds the redemption to come.

Tablets of the Covenant

The 'Tablets of the Covenant', or 'Tablets of Testimony', often also called 'Tables of the Law', were presented for the first time by God to Moses on Mount Sinai. The work of the Everlasting God (Exod 32:16), written with his finger (Exod 31:18), these stone tablets were smashed by the prophet when he discovered that in his absence Israel had indulged in worship of the Golden Calf (Exod 32:19). Once the people had been chastised, Moses carved two new tablets and re-ascended Sinai. At God's dictation, he himself engraved 'the words of the covenant, the ten commandments' (Exod 34:28). These second tablets were subsequently deposited in the Ark of the Covenant (or Ark of the Testimony) placed at the heart of the mobile desert sanctuary (Exod 25), and then in the holy of holies in the Temple of Jerusalem, privileged site of the manifestation of the divine Presence among his chosen people. The travels of this ark and its contents give rise to miracles in several biblical stories, such as the parting of the waters of the River Jordan (Josh 3–4) and the destruction of the walls of Jericho (Josh 6). With the ruin of the first Temple in 586 BCE, they disappeared for ever. On account of their great symbolic value, the tablets – their material, dimensions, form, weight and content – have been the subject of many Midrashic discussions. According to some traditions, they were among the things created on the eve of the first Shabbat of Creation and, in addition to the Decalogue, are said to have contained the 613 commandments or even the entire oral Law.

Talmud

From the Hebrew word for 'study, instruction'. Commentary on the Mishnah produced by the masters of the academies of Palestine and Babylon. There are two Talmuds. The so-called Jerusalem Talmud was hastily compiled in Tiberias towards the end of the fourth century. The Babylonian Talmud was gradually laid down, its definitive format having been initiated by Rav Ashi (352–427), head of the Sura Academy, and completed by one of his successors, Ravina II (d. 499). The Babylonian Talmud's authority eventually became established throughout the Jewish world.

Targum

From the Hebrew word for 'translation'. Term referring specifically to the ancient Aramaic translations of the Bible. After Aramaic had become the vernacular language of Jews in Babylonia and then Palestine, the custom spread of translating and interpreting in this idiom the text of the Pentateuch and the passages from the Prophets ritually read during the synagogal service. Far from always being literal, these translations often took the form of paraphrases and Midrashic developments. Reading the *targumim* was a constant source of inspiration to the great medieval Jewish commentators.

Torah

From the Hebrew. Derived from a verb meaning 'to guide, to instruct', this noun, often narrowly rendered as 'Law', can equally refer to a particular legal disposition and the whole of the divine message transmitted to Israel through the intermediary of Moses. The Jewish tradition thus calls 'Torah of Moses' what we call the Pentateuch, the first and most venerated of the three elements making up the Hebrew Bible. By extension, the word has come to refer to the set of normative teachings of Judaism, not only the written Torah but also the oral Torah. In fact, everything falls under this name: Bible, Mishnah, Talmud, rabbinical literature in all its forms, and so forth.

Indicative Bibliography

Ahad Ha'am, 'Moses', in *Complete Works*, 8th printing, Tel Aviv and Jerusalem, 1964–65, 342–47 (in Hebrew).

Alter, Robert. *The Five Books of Moses: A Translation with Commentary* (1st. ed.), New York: W.W. Norton & Company, 2004.

Alter, Robert and Kermode, Frank, eds, *The Literary Guide to the Bible*, Cambridge, MA: Harvard University Press, 1990.

Amir-Moezzi, Mohammad Ali, ed., *Dictionnaire du Coran*, Paris: Robert Laffont, 2007.

Asch, Sholem, *Moses*, trans. Maurice Samuel, New York: Putnam, 1951.

Assmann, Jan, *Moses the Egyptian: The Memory of Egypt in Western Monotheism*, Cambridge, MA: Harvard University Press, 1997.

Attias, Jean-Christophe, *The Jews and the Bible*, trans. Patrick Camiller, Stanford, CA: Stanford University Press, 2015.

——, 'Enfants sans pères: Jésus et "le fils de la femme israélite"', in Jean-Christophe Attias, *Penser le judaïsme*, Paris: CNRS Éditions, 2013, 241–54.

—, '"Moïse ignorait que la peau de son visage était cornue." Lectures d'Exode 34, 29–35', in Attias, *Penser le judaïsme*, Paris: CNRS Éditions, 2013, 157–83.

Berlin, Adele, Brettler, Mark Zvi, Fishbane, Michael and Jewish Publication Society, *The Jewish Study Bible: Jewish Publication Society Tanakh Translation*, Oxford and New York: Oxford University Press, 2004.

Borgeaud, Philippe, Römer, Thomas and Volokhine, Youri, *Interprétations de Moïse*, Égypte, Judée, Grèce et Rome, Leiden and Boston: Brill, 2010.

Buber, Martin, *Moses: The Revelation and the Covenant*, Atlantic Highland, NJ: Humanities Press, 1988.

Chapitres de Rabbi Éliézer, trans. from the Hebrew and annotated by Marc-Alain Ouaknin and Éric Smilévitch, new revised and corrected edition, Lagrasse: Verdier, 1992.

Chouraqui, André, *Moïse. Voyages aux confins d'un mystère révélé et d'une utopie réalisable*, Paris: Éditions du Rocher, 1995.

Cohen, Shaye J. D., *Why aren't Jewish women circumcised? Gender and Covenant in Judaism*, Berkeley: University of California Press, 2005.

Danziger, Raymond, *L'Énigme du rocher. La disgrâce de Moïse*, Paris: Lichma, 2012.

Edelman, Diana V., Davies, Philip R., Nihan, Christophe and Römer, Thomas, *Opening the Books of Moses*, Routledge: Abingdon and New York, 2014.

Flavius Josephus, 'The Antiquities of the Jews', in *The Complete Works*, trans. William Whiston, Nashville: Thomas Nelson, 1998.

Fleg, Edmond, *The Life of Moses*, trans. Stephen Haden Guest, London: Gollancz, 1928.

Freud, Sigmund, 'The Moses of Michelangelo', trans. James Strachey, in *Totem and Taboo and Other Works (1913–1914)*, London: Hogarth Press/The Institute of Psychoanalysis, 1955.

——, 'Moses and Monotheism', trans. James Strachey, in *Moses and Monotheism, An Outline of Psychoanalysis and Other Works (1937–1939)*, London: Hogarth Press/The Institute of Psychoanalysis, 1955.

Ginzberg, Louis, *Legends of the Jews*, vol. 1, books VII–XI, Philadelphia: Jewish Publication Society, 2003.

Goldstein, Bluma, *Reinscribing Moses: Heine, Kafka, Freud and Schoenberg in a European Wilderness*, Cambridge, MA: Harvard University Press, 1992.

Gregory of Nyssa, *The Life of Moses*, trans. Abraham J. Malherbe and Everett Ferguson, New York: HarperCollins, 2006.

Karsenti, Bruno, *Moïse et l'idée du peuple. La vérité historique selon Freud*, Paris: Cerf, 2012.

Korczak, Janusz, *Moïse, le Benjamin de la Bible*, French text by Zofia Bobowicz, Troyes: Librairie Bleue/UNESCO, 1988.

Kugel, James L., *How to Read the Bible: A Guide to Scripture, Then and Now*, New York: Free Press, 2008.

La Bible, translated and introduced by André Chouraqui, new ed., Paris: Desclée de Brouwer, 1989.

Leçons des Pères du monde. Pirké Avot et Avot de Rabbi Nathan Version A et B, trans. from the Hebrew by Éric Smilévitch, Lagrasse: Verdier, 1983.

Luciani, Didier, 'Cippora (Ex 4, 24-26): un oiseau qui s'échappe du filet des interprètes', in Régis Burnet and Didier Luciani, eds, *La Circoncision. Parcours biblique*, Brussels: Lessius, 2013.

Maimonides, Moses, *The Guide of the Perplexed*, 2 vols, trans. Shlomo Pines, Chicago and London: University of Chicago Press, 1963.

Mann, Thomas, *The Tables of the Law* (1st Paul Dry Books ed.), trans. by Marion Faber and Stephen Lehmann, Philadelphia: Paul Dry Books, 2010.

Neher, André, *Moïse et la vocation juive*, Paris: Éditions du Seuil, 1956.

Origen, *Homélies sur l'Exode*, Latin text introduced and annotated by Marcel Borret, Paris: Cerf, 1985.

Le Pentateuque . . ., *accompagné du commentaire de Rachi*, Hebrew-French bilingual edition, 5 vols, edited by Élie Munk, Paris: Fondation Samuel and Odette Lévy, 1987.

Philo of Alexandria, 'On the Life of Moses', trans. C.D. Yonge, in *The Works of Philo*, Peabody, MA: Hendrickson Publishers, 2013.

Rad, Gerhard von, *Moses*, trans. Stephen Nell and ed. K.C. Hanson, (2nd ed.) Eugene, OR: Cascade Books, 2011.

Römer, Thomas, *The Horns of Moses: Setting the Bible in Its Historical Context*, trans. Liz Libbrecht, Paris: Collège de France/OpenEdition Books, 2013.

——, *Moïse en version originale*, Paris: Bayard, 2015.

——, *Moïse, 'lui que Yahvé a connu face à face'*, Paris: Gallimard, 2002.

Rozier, Gilles, *Moïse fiction*, Paris: Denoël, 2001.

Schlegel, Jean-Louis, *Moïse et le Dieu unique. Aux fondements du monothéisme*, Paris: Hatier, 2013.

Schoenberg, Arnold, *Moïse et Aaron*, *L'Avant-Scène Opéra*, no. 167, September–October 1995.

Silver, Daniel Jeremy, *Images of Moses*, New York: Basic Books, 1982.

Skali, Faouzi, *Moïse dans la tradition soufie*, Paris: Albin Michel, 2011.

Szlakmann, Charles, *Moïse*, Paris: Gallimard, 2009.

Targum du Pentateuque, translation of two complete Palestinian recensions, with introduction, parallels, notes and index, by Roger Le Déaut in collaboration with Jacques Robert, 5 vols, Paris: Cerf, 1980–2008.

Vigny, Alfred de, 'Moïse', 1822, in *Poèmes antiques et modernes. Les Destinées*, Paris: Poésie/Gallimard, 1973, 19–22.

Voltaire, 'Moses', in *A Pocket Philosophical Dictionary*, trans. John Fletcher, Oxford: Oxford University Press, 2011.

Yerushalmi, Yosef Hayim, *Freud's 'Moses': Judaism Terminable and Interminable*, New Haven: Yale University Press, 1991.

Acknowledgements

This book is primarily the fruit of a happy encounter between a request and a suggestion. Jean-Maurice de Montremy, a publisher but above all a very old friend, asked me for a book for Alma Éditeur, which he had just set up with Catherine Argand. Concurrently, my long-time partner, Prof. Esther Benbassa, suggested a subject: Moses. I put up some token resistance. And then, having agreed to sign a contract, I dawdled for as long as I could. Not only for bad reasons. This Moses: I didn't in fact know how to approach him. In my seminar at the École pratique des hautes études (PSL University), I tried out various possible angles. And I finally got down to writing this book. It bears little resemblance to my initial concept or to the proposal I'd submitted to my publisher. For the project to come to fruition, some tenacity was required on the part of Jean-Maurice de Montremy, along with much patience and a good deal of trust. I can only thank him once more wholeheartedly. I dare to hope that Esther Benbassa, who is not only my companion, but also an experienced historian and my first reader, forgives me for having produced a text that is obviously much less a scholarly essay than a literary, even 'theological', exercise.

Naturally, I cannot end these acknowledgements without mentioning the EPHE's Alberto Benveniste Centre for Sephardic Studies and Jewish Socio-Cultural History, which has hosted and generously supported my work since its foundation in 2001. Like many others, I am grateful to it for the freedom and comfort – rare in the French university system – it vouchsafes its researchers. A word of sincere gratitude too for the Centre Roland-Mousnier (UMR 8596 – CNRS/Université Paris-Sorbonne/EPHE), to which the Centre Alberto Benveniste is attached, and for its successive directors, Prof. Denis Crouzet and Prof. Cyril Grange, who have succeeded in cultivating there an atmosphere of healthy emulation and genuine tolerance.

Finally, thank you to Sebastian Budgen of Verso who has been unstinting in his efforts to make this publication in English possible, as well as the Centre National du Livre (CNL, Paris), which agreed to support it financially. Thanks to the fine work of my translator, Gregory Elliott, and the expertise of my copy editor, Lorna Scott Fox, *Moïse fragile*, which has become *A Woman Called Moses*, will have safely crossed waters that are no doubt less familiar to him than those of the Red Sea.

Notes

The Life of Moses according to the Pentateuch

1 Corresponding to the traditional Jewish identification of Jacob with the Jews and of Esau with Rome and Christianity is the identification by Christian authors of Jacob with the Church and Esau with Judaism.

1 The Prophet's Wounded Body

1 In Hebrew, *kol demamah dakkah*. Here, as in all quotations from the Bible, the emphasis is mine.

2 Recently, Ridley Scott, with his *Exodus: Gods and Kings*, has not done any better; he has probably done worse. Spectacular, violent, characterized by a glazed aestheticism and chilling 'realism', his film only gains as much in profundity as is to be anticipated from 3D. Hardly more. Scott's bellicose Moses is not even the 'schizophrenic barbarian' whom the actor playing him – Christian Bale – has claimed to see in him.

3 Sigmund Freud, 'The Moses of Michelangelo', trans. James Strachey, in *Totem and Taboo and Other Works*, London: Hogarth Press/ Institute of Psychoanalysis, 1955, p. 233.

4 I shall return to this below, pp. 138–146 .

5 Philo of Alexandria, *On the Life of Moses*, I:9.

6 Gregory of Nyssa, *The Life of Moses*, I:16.

7 Sholem Asch, *Moses*, trans. Maurice Samuel, New York: Putnam, 1951, p. 51.

8 Ibid., pp. 407–8.

9 Gregory of Nyssa, *Life of Moses*, 2:319.

10 Philo, *On the Life of Moses*, I:158.

11 Ahad Ha'am, 'Moses', in *Complete Works*, Tel Aviv: Jerusalem, 1964–5 (in Hebrew), p. 342.

12 Ibid., p. 343.

13 Before Palestine became fixed upon as the sole country capable of assembling scattered Jewry, other possibilities were envisaged: Uganda (in reality Kenya), Argentina, Madagascar, and even New Caledonia. Theodor Herzl, the founder of political Zionism, himself briefly rallied to the Ugandan solution. It was only after his death in 1904 that his successors unconditionally opted for Palestine.

14 Arnold Schoenberg, *Moses and Aaron*, Act II, scene 4.

15 See Rashi on Exodus 4:16.

16 Flavius Josephus, *The Antiquities of the Jews*, V:1 and IV: 326.

17 Sifre on Deuteronomy, 375:5.

18 Mishnah, Avot, 5:6.

19 See Asch, *Moses*, p. 5.

20 Philo, *On the Life of Moses*, I:83.

21 Ibid., I:84.

22 I shall return to this curious episode in Chapter 3.

23 *Pirkei de-Rabbi Eliezer*, 48.

24 See below, pp. 55–6.
25 *Avot de-Rabbi Nathan* A, 2.

2 The Egyptian Woman's Son

1 The word 'mosaic', referring to an art, derives from the Greek. It has nothing to do with Moses etymologically, but refers to the Muses.
2 See Rashi on Genesis 17:5,15.
3 See Babylonian Talmud, *Sotah*, 12a.
4 See Rashi on Exodus 2:1-10.
5 See *Hizkuni* on this verse.
6 Leviticus Rabbah, 1:3.
7 See pp. 22–3.
8 *Pirkei de-Rabbi Eliezer*, 48.
9 Leviticus Rabbah, 1:3.
10 Babylonian Talmud, *Megillah*, 13a.
11 Babylonian Talmud, *Sanhedrin*, 19b.
12 See Rashi on Exodus 2:16.
13 See Exodus Rabbah, 27:2.
14 He will behave still 'worse' later, with a second marriage to 'an Ethiopian woman', no less (Num 12:1). A Black wife! Might this be the last scriptural vestige of the campaign which, according to non-biblical sources, Moses conducted in Ethiopia on behalf of Pharaoh? Needless to say, the rabbinical tradition bends over backwards to neutralize the episode: the Ethiopian woman is none other than Zipporah herself. But why, in that case, is she referred to thus? 'Ethiopian' here is merely another way of saying 'beautiful'. The letters that form the word *Kushit* (Ethiopian woman) have the same numerical value (736) as those forming the phrase *yefat mar'eh* (of beautiful appearance). Everyone acknowledged Zipporah's beauty, just as everyone agrees about the blackness of an Ethiopian.

And calling her 'Black' was a way of deflecting the evil eye from her (see Sifre Deuteronomy and Rashi on this passage).

15 *Mekhilta de-Rabbi Yishma'el, Yitro,* 1.

16 Exodus Rabbah, 1:32.

17 See, in particular, Leviticus Rabbah, 1:28-29 and Rashi on the two relevant passages.

18 Three words in Hebrew, whose initials make up the name *Ye-SH-U*: **Y**imah **Sh**emo **V**e-zikhro (erased be his name and his memory).

3 Journey, Night, Death

1 Robert Alter, *The Five Books of Moses: A Translation with Commentary* (1st. ed.), New York: W.W. Norton & Company, 2004, 330-32.

2 This is our English translation of Chouraqui's own French (and very literal) translation from the Hebrew (*La Bible,* new ed., Paris: Desclée de Brouwer, 1989, 122). In French: 'Et c'est sur la route, au gîte: IHVH le rencontre, il cherche à le faire mourir. Şipora prend un silex, tranche le prépuce de son fils et avec le touche à ses pieds. Elle dit: "Oui, tu es pour moi un époux de sang." Il le relâche. Alors elle dit: "Un époux de sang, par les circoncisions!"'

3 See above, p. 40.

4 I emphasize what the Targum adds to the verse.

5 The end of Exodus 4:26, rewritten by Neofiti 1.

6 And, before him, the Babylonian Talmud, *Nedarim* 31b–32a.

7 See below, pp. 116–20.

8 The same formula as appears right at the start of our narrative: 'As he was *on the way* [*ba-derekh*] . . .' (Exod 4:24).

9 Babylonian Talmud, *Nedarim,* 32a.

10 For the word *satan* is used twice in the text (Num 22: 22, 32), and can take any of these three meanings. For a clearly 'Satanic' *satan,* authorized by God to put a righteous man to the test, see Job 1:6–12.

11 The text employs a verb constructed from the root *ng'* (touch, hit, wound). The verb that will later be used to refer to Zipporah's action after the circumcision of her son is constructed from the same root. But it involves a transitive: 'she *made* [it] *touch* his feet' (Exod 4:25).

4 A Woman Called Moses

1 In the Jewish calendar, the day begins at sunset and ends the following day at sunset, in accordance with the formula of Genesis 1:5: 'And the evening and the morning were the first day'.

2 *Sivan* is the month of the Hebrew calendar corresponding to May–June and, according to Tradition, that of the revelation on Sinai. On 6 *sivan*, seven weeks after Passover, the Jewish festival of *Shavu'ot* ('Weeks') is celebrated, commemorating the bestowal of the Torah on Sinai.

3 *Tammuz* is the Jewish month corresponding to June–July. In the liturgical calendar, 17 *tammuz* is a day of fasting that commemorates both the first breach made in the walls of Jerusalem by Nebuchadnezzar, one 9 *tammuz*, before the destruction of the First Temple; and the first breach made in the outer wall of the city, one 17 *tammuz*, before the destruction of the Second Temple. But according to Jewish tradition, several other negative events occurred on the same date – among them the destruction of the first Tables of the Law by Moses (as we shall see), and the suspension of the daily burnt offering in the Temple during the Roman siege of Jerusalem.

4 I emphasize what the Targum adds to the text of Scripture.

5 *Targum du Pentateuque*, vol. 2, Add. 27031, p. 249 and 251.

6 Rabbinical sources play here on the verb *boshesh* ('delayed'), which appears in Exodus 32:1, breaking it down thus: *ba'u* (have passed) *shesh* (six [hours]).

7 Rashi and Babylonian Talmud, *Shabbat*, 89a.

8 According to a Midrashic story, Nimrod, a king who worshipped fire, threw Abraham into a furnace because he refused to renounce the One God. The patriarch emerged miraculously safe and sound.

9 Allusion to the sacrifice of Isaac as related in Genesis 22.

10 Exodus Rabbah, 44:5 and Rashi on this passage. Jacob was exiled at the request of his father Isaac, in order to find a wife (Genesis 28).

11 *Yeshua*, or *Yehoshua*, a name that in the language of the Bible, far from evoking a curse, actually evokes salvation (literally: God saves). Such is the name of Jesus: 'thou shalt call his name Jesus: for he shall save his people from their sins' (Matt 1:21). And, before him, it is also that of Joshua, Moses's successor.

12 *Yeshua* or *Yehoshua* becoming simply *YeSHU*, written *yod-shin-vav*, these three letters being construed (as we have seen) as an abbreviation of **Yimmah Shemo Ve-zikhro**.

13 Babylonian Talmud, *Berakhot*, 32a and Rashi on this passage.

14 I emphasize what Nachmanides' commentary adds to the verse to spell out its meaning.

15 *Mekhilta de-Rabbi Yishma'el, Bo, Masekhta de-Pas'ha* 1.

16 Babylonian Talmud, *Sanhedrin*, 102a.

17 Babylonian Talmud, *Shabbat*, 87a.

18 Moses supposedly reasoned as follows: for the single hour for which the divine Presence addressed Israel during the theophany on Sinai, three days of prior chastity had been prescribed to the people (see Exodus 19:10–11). Consequently, the same principle should apply with even greater strictness when the divine Presence was talking to him constantly, without appointing a time.

19 See above, p. 50. On the second wife, see above, p. 179 n. 14.

20 See Exodus 4:22: 'Thus saith the Lord, Israel is my son, even my firstborn.'

21 'You make an *at*, a "feminine you", of me.'

22 We saw above (pp. 78–9 that they ended up believing the fire had indeed consumed him.

23 In the original account of this episode in the Book of Exodus, the Hebrews employ the pronoun in the masculine: 'Speak thou [*ata*] with us' (Exod 20:19).

24 Babylonian Talmud, *Berakhot*, 32a.

5 Divine Snares

1 'My spirit shall not always strive with man . . . his days shall be an hundred and twenty years' (Gen 6:3). In fact, according to more than one commentator, these 'hundred and twenty years' are simply the period of time allowed the generation of the Flood by God to repent before his fury is unleashed.

2 By contrast, it was Moses himself who removed the bones of Joseph, in accordance with the latter's request, at the time of the Exodus (Exod 13:19). They were finally buried in Shechem, in a piece of land acquired by Jacob (Josh 24:32).

3 Rashi and Babylonian Talmud, *Bava Batra*, 15a.

4 Sifre on Deuteronomy, 357:2.

5 Babylonian Talmud, *Berakhot*,18b, and Rashi on this passage.

6 This is almost a habit, as will have been noted. The bargain is identical to the one offered to Moses – and refused by him in the same way – after the transgression of the Golden Calf (see above pp. 81–83).

7 Sifre on Deuteronomy, 21:23.

8 Rashi on this passage.

9 See Rashi on this passage and its sources.

10 Rashbam on Numbers 20:10.

11 Ibid.

12 See Numbers 27:12–14: 'And the Lord said unto Moses, Get thee up into this mount Abarim, and see the land which I have given

unto the children of Israel. And when thou hast seen it, thou also shalt be gathered unto thy people, as Aaron thy brother was gathered. For ye rebelled against my commandment in the desert of Zin, in the strife of the congregation, to sanctify me at the water before their eyes: that is the water of Meribah in Kadesh in the wilderness of Zin.'

13 Rashi on this passage.

14 Babylonian Talmud, *Ta'anit*, 9a.

15 Rashi on this passage.

16 *Tanhuma, Hukkat*, 9.

17 Babylonian Talmud, *Mo'ed Katan*, 28a.

18 Gregory of Nyssa, *Life of Moses*, 2:136.

19 Babylonian Talmud, *Bava Kama*, 17a.

20 See Babylonian Talmud, *Sotah*, 13b.

6 Light and Shadow

1 Mishnah, *Avot*, 1:1.

2 An institution which, according to rabbinical tradition, formed the link between the Prophets and the first representative of the Pharisaic tradition (Simeon the Just).

3 *Tanhuma, Va-yera*, 5.

4 In Hebrew *meshihai*, which is the plural, augmented by the first person singular of the possessive pronoun, of *mashiah*, 'messiah'. Literally 'anointed', and here, 'mine anointed'.

5 Babylonian Talmud, *Shabbat*, 119b.

6 Founder of Mormonism (1805–1844), recipient of various visions and revelations, to whom we owe in particular *The Book of Mormon*, a volume of sacred writings to be added to the Old and New Testaments.

7 In the course of a citation from Exodus 14:31 that is far from doing justice to the prophet. This is itself absent from some manuscripts.

8 Moses Maimonides, *The Guide of the Perplexed*, I.39.

9 Abraham Ibn Ezra on Deuteronomy 5:4.

10 Rashi on Deuteronomy 34:10.

11 Rashi on Babylonian Talmud, *Yevamot*, 49b.

12 Babylonian Talmud, 49b and Leviticus Rabbah, 1:13.

13 The verb *karan* seems to be based on the same root as the word *keren* which, in biblical Hebrew, always has the meaning of 'horn', a symbol of power, and assumes that of 'ray' only in post-biblical Hebrew. Rashi attempts a reconciliation by suggesting that the light shining from Moses's face projected its brilliance 'like a kind of horn'.

14 Maimonides, *Guide of the Perplexed*, Introduction.

15 *Zohar*, I:31b–32a.

16 *Hizkuni* on Exodus 34:29.

17 Origen, *Homilies on Exodus*, XII.

18 Compare Mark 9:2–4 and Luke 9:28–30.

19 Saadia Gaon cited by Abraham Ibn Ezra, long commentary on Numbers 34:34.

20 Rashi on Numbers 34:33–35.

21 Abraham Ibn Ezra, long commentary on Numbers 34:34.

22 Babylonian Talmud, *Bava Metsia*, 59b.

23 Abraham Ibn Ezra, short commentary on Numbers 34:33–35.

24 In his long commentary on Numbers 34:34.

25 Pierre Lory, 'Moïse', in Mohammad Ali Amir-Moezzi, ed., *Dictionnaire du Coran*, Paris: Robert Laffont, 2007, p. 558.

26 That is, in accordance with God's purpose for him, the role that God intended to have him play.

27 In fact, the rabbinical literature relates a rather similar tale to that of the Qur'an, where it is Elijah who plays the role of initiating master, and Joshua ben Levi, a third-century Jewish sage, that of the bad disciple. In truth, this narrative framework is evidently

transcultural and, down to Voltaire in Chapter 20 of *Zadig*, many have sought to recycle it. There it is Zadig who plays the role of disciple and a mysterious hermit that of master.

28 In Hebrew: '*halakhah le-Mosheh mi-Sinai*'; literally, 'a law to Moses from Sinai'.

29 Babylonian Talmud, *Menahot*, 29b.

30 See above, pp. 98 and 100.

31 Moses is actually only one of four great figures who died at the age of 120. If Sifre Deuteronomy, 357:7 is to be believed, three sages had the same privilege, including Rabbi Akiba.

Conclusion

1 A rabbinical expression applied to religious rules or provisions whose support in Scripture is extremely tenuous, albeit real.

2 See above p. 2.

3 See Abraham Ibn Ezra on Job 4:16 and Gersonides on I Kings 19:12.

4 According to Deuteronomy 26:5.

5 Babylonian Talmud, *Bava Batra*, 75a.

Index